AN INCONVENIENT FLAME

LOVE IN THE ADIRONDACKS

JEN TALTY

JUPITER PRESS

This book is a work of fiction. Names, characters, places, and incidents are products of the author's imagination or used fictitiously. Any resemblance to actual events or locales or persons living or dead is entirely coincidental.

Copyright © 2021 by Jen Talty All rights reserved.

No part of this work may be used, stored, reproduced or transmitted without written permission from the publisher except for brief quotations for review purposes as permitted by law.

This book is licensed for your personal enjoyment only. This book may not be re-sold or given away to other people. If you would like to share this book with another person, please purchase an additional copy for each recipient. If you're reading this book and did not purchase it, or it was not purchased for your use only, please purchase your own copy.

AN INCONVENIENT FLAME
LOVE IN THE ADIRONDACKS, BOOK 1

USA Today Bestseller
JEN TALTY

PRAISE FOR JEN TALTY

"Deadly Secrets is the best of romance and suspense in one hot read!" *NYT Bestselling Author Jennifer Probst*

"A charming setting and a steamy couple heat up the pages in a suspenseful story I couldn't put down!" *NY Times and USA today Bestselling Author Donna Grant*

"Jen Talty's books will grab your attention and pull you into a world of relatable characters, strong personalities, humor, and believable storylines. You'll laugh, you'll cry, and you'll rush to get the next book she releases!" Natalie Ann USA Today Bestselling Author

"I positively loved *In Two Weeks*, and highly recommend it. The writing is wonderful, the story is fantastic, and the characters will keep you coming back for more. I can't wait to get my hands on future installments of the NYS Troopers series." *Long and Short Reviews*

"*In Two Weeks* hooks the reader from page one. This is a fast paced story where the development of the romance grabs you emotionally and the suspense keeps you sitting on the edge of your chair. Great characters, great writing, and a believable plot that can be a warning to all of us." *Desiree Holt, USA Today Bestseller*

"*Dark Water* delivers an engaging portrait of wounded hearts as the memorable characters take you on a healing journey of love. A mysterious death brings danger and intrigue into the drama, while sultry passions brew into a believable plot that melts the reader's heart. Jen Talty pens an entertaining romance that grips the heart as the colorful and dangerous story unfolds into a chilling ending." *Night Owl Reviews*

"This is not the typical love story, nor is it the typical mystery. The characters are well rounded and interesting." *You Gotta Read Reviews*

"Murder in Paradise Bay is a fast-paced romantic thriller with plenty of twists and turns to keep you guessing until the end. You won't want to miss this one..." USA Today bestselling author Janice Maynard

BOOK DESCRIPTION

The last thing she wanted was a man. But he was exactly what she needed.

Tayla Johnson doesn't have time for romance. She barely has time to stop and smell the roses. However, when her parents plan a big family reunion, she makes a promise to her mom and dad she will take two weeks off work and spend time with them and her two sisters. Something she hasn't done in years. She's ready for a little fun in her childhood home, but she's not prepared for the sexy next-door neighbor that won't take no for an answer. She doesn't want love or happily-ever-after. All she's ever known is work, career, and sheer determination.

Gael Waylen spent most of his twenties and thirties chasing dollar signs. He had no idea life had passed him by until his parents and baby sister were killed in a small plane crash six months ago. At their funeral, he vowed to make changes in his life, but he has no idea what that really looked like until the day Tayla Johnson came home. He sees in her exactly who he used to be and he doesn't want her to make the same mistakes. While he tells himself he's only trying to give her the gift of time, he ends up giving her his heart.

To memories of childhood.

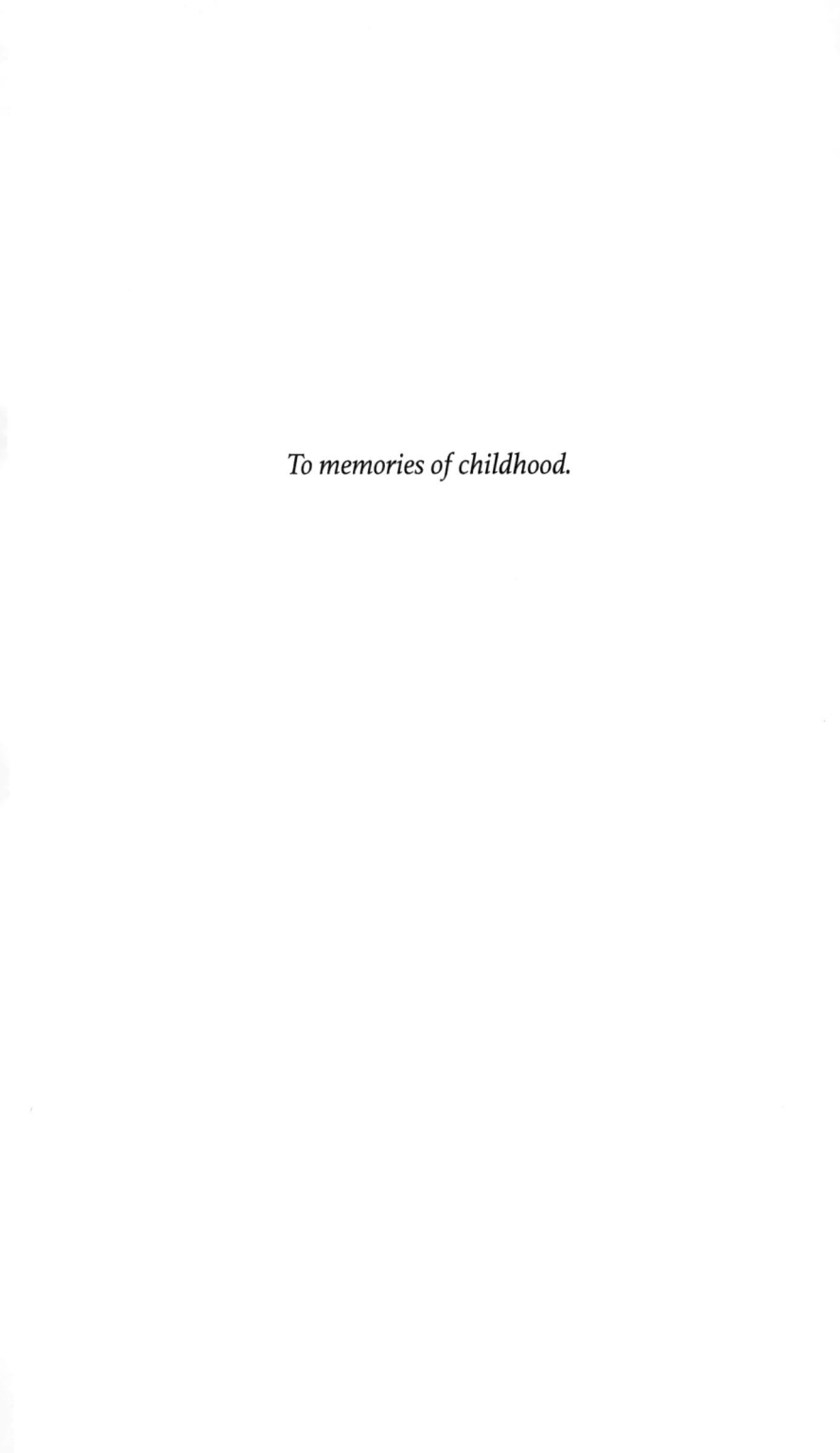

1

"I just have to stop at the corner store." Tayla Johnson gripped the steering wheel and punched the gas. Every time she left New York City, her heart raced, and not because she was excited. Or because she was looking forward to getting away from the hustle and bustle for a few days. Or even the fact she was going back to her hometown of Lake George to see her sisters and her parents.

Though, that should be the reason.

She loved her family. They meant the world to her, and she would do just about anything for them. She wanted to spend more time with her sisters. With her parents.

And especially with her grandfather, while he

was in good health. He wasn't getting any younger, and she knew his days were numbered. She would never tell him that she thought that though. He'd be mortified.

However, the reality was that she knew her family would give her shit, and she either needed to come up with a really good reason for why she was late or face the firing squad.

"That doesn't answer my question," Tiki, one of her younger sisters, said.

Tayla glanced at the clock. "I'm three minutes from the turn," she said. That should calm Tiki down, but it did nothing to make Tayla feel better about the situation. She was coming home. It should be enough. But she knew that wasn't the case.

While Tayla loved her family and looked forward to spending time with them, nothing about leaving her life in the city appealed to her in any way, shape, or form. Not because her life was that thrilling, but because everything she'd worked for was in New York City.

It was the fashion capital of this half of the world, and she was on her way to breaking out of the pack.

Or so she hoped.

But it was more than that.

Leaving meant not being under the watchful eye of her boss, Anna Declay, one of the world's most popular and sought-after designers, and Tayla was lucky enough to be working under Anna's tutelage.

Although lately, she felt as though someone had tied a noose around her neck. But that would change. She'd make sure of it. As soon as Anna launched a line with Tayla's name, Tayla would be able to put in her notice. But until then, she was Anna's girl.

Or as everyone in the office called it: *Anna's bitch.*

Whatever. Tayla didn't care. She did her best to let the jealousy and all the dirty snickers roll off her back. Everyone in this business had to sell their soul a little bit. The ones who didn't, well, the world never heard their name.

That wasn't going to be Tayla. Not now. She was the one Anna whispered to during fashion shows. The one Anna texted when she had a question or wanted an opinion about what another designer had done. Tayla held the spot that every other thirsty designer coveted and would do just about anything to have.

Including sabotage.

And if they told anyone otherwise, they were liars.

Or simply not ambitious.

Which meant Tayla's world could change in the blink of an eye. Tayla saw it happen three times in the last year. The old saying *if you snooze, you lose* was never truer. The entire reason she was in the position of Anna's right hand was because the three people before her weren't willing to sell their firstborn child to the highest bidder to stay on Anna's radar.

Well, Tayla didn't have kids.

She didn't have a boyfriend.

Hell, she barely had friends.

She'd set all that aside to make this dream come true. The rest could happen as soon as this part of her life was settled.

She lived for her career, and right now, her career was Anna Declay Designs.

When Tayla first took the job with Anna, the goal had been for Anna to recognize how truly talented Tayla was and to give her the opportunity to prove herself. Not just use her gifts so the Anna name could shine at every major fashion event. So far, not one single designer working for Anna had been given that privilege.

Tayla had decided she would be the first to punch through the ranks. That alone would give her the foothold she needed to be different. To stand out where others blended in with the pack. So, when she did leave Anna Declay Designs, it wouldn't matter what Anna said or did. Tayla would have street credibility. She would have arrived. This was a means to an end.

She just needed to navigate through the maze.

It wasn't an unreasonable path to her dream either. A gown she'd created under the direction of Anna had been worn by a famous actress last holiday season on the red carpet. The actress made a big deal about how Anna had designed it just for her and when the reporters asked Anna about it, the answer had shocked the world.

Anna Declay had stated she worked with someone else to come up with an incredible masterpiece. An up-and-coming artist whom Anna wasn't prepared to mention by name yet because she knew when she did, every designer was going to want to snatch *her* for themselves and Anna wasn't about to let that happen. However, the designer needed more time to develop and hone her skills while creating a line specific for Anna Declay Designs.

Those had been Anna's words.

When Tayla heard them, her body tingled with the kind of excitement that only happens when dreams were about to materialize. Unfortunately, that sensation only lasted a few moments as she reminded herself of how things worked in the land of Anna. She teased you. Dangled the carrot. Anna made you chase it in ways that most people would walk away from.

Anna more than made a person work for the right to have their name recognized. She made you grovel for it and sometimes it didn't feel good. But Tayla had been working for this moment since she could remember. Giving up now when she'd been so close didn't make sense. Not to mention Anna would crush her reputation like a bug.

"I wanted to talk to you and Tonya before we sat down to dinner," Tiki said. Of her two younger sisters, Tiki was the middle child. Growing up, she'd been the one who had no use for a boyfriend because she was too busy having a good time. She wasn't a party girl, but she enjoyed her freedom. Not to mention she was the fickle one and the one most likely to be distracted by the next attractive man who walked into her life.

But she'd fallen head over heels in love with Josh and now, Tiki thought she had the perfect little life with her job as a paralegal and the perfect man who was probably going to propose at any time.

Tayla wanted to gag. Not literally, of course.

She was happy for her sister, but no one really liked Josh. He didn't fit in with the rest of the family and never tried. He tended to keep everyone at arm's length and that didn't go over well.

"I'll be there in ten minutes. Dinner's not for a couple of hours."

"I told you that I had an appointment. I'm heading out now. You'll pass me on the road," Tiki said.

"I had a lot of things to do at the office before I left," Tayla said. She hated that she once again had disappointed her sister. Her family. But it couldn't be helped. She had to secure this part of her career. If she didn't, she might as well pack up and go home.

"I get that, but you told me the last time we spoke you were taking the day off. Not the afternoon off. I've been sitting around waiting for you. The least you could have done was respond to some of my texts."

Tayla's chest tightened. She'd been so caught up in her own shit, she'd completely forgotten. "I'm sorry. I had to finish up some loose ends if I was going to take a vacation. I explained all this to Mom and Dad, and I should be there before Mom would consider me late." She'd kept mentally reminding herself before she left the office to text her sister, but until Tiki called five minutes ago, her mind had been on work. Not family. That was exactly the kind of thing everyone had been bugging her about.

In her mind, this period in her life was temporary.

A short-term situation to reach a long-term goal.

"Well, she's already complaining that you're not here," Tiki said. "I have to run. Josh is calling."

Before Tayla could say another word, the phone went dead. Lately, Tiki had been acting strange. Tayla couldn't put her finger on what it was, but her sister hadn't been herself the last few times they'd spoken. She'd been quick to argue. As a matter of fact, Tayla felt like every time they did speak, it was as if Tiki wanted to fight.

Tayla's heart beat faster as she approached Cleverdale Road and the Country Store. While a lot had changed over the years, so much had remained the same. The firehouse still stood tall and proud across the street. Behind it was a playground. When she'd been a little girl, it had an old metal slide. About ten years ago, that had been replaced with a big yellow plastic one along with a new bigger and better sandbox and swing set.

The convenience store had an addition, but was

the same log cabin style, though there was no longer gas available. She parked in front of the new building, admiring how well it matched the old one.

The new shop was where customers could pick up shirts, sweatshirts, signs, and even hiking equipment. The owners had separated out what would be considered tourist-type trinkets or hikers' desires from the daily shopping needs of the locals.

She did her best to ignore the little voice in her head that begged her to turn the car around and hightail it back to the city. For the first time since taking the job with Anna Declay Designs, she had a real chance at having her own line. This was not the time for Tayla to be playing hooky. Her muscles twitched as she snagged her purse from the passenger seat. She took in a deep breath, reminding herself she was on vacation and that Anna herself signed off on it. Anna had whispered in her ear during a creative meeting how utterly bored she'd been with everyone's designs—except Tayla's and how she wished she could hightail it to Lake George and take a mini vacation. Later that day, Anna called Tayla into her office and demanded Tayla take that vacation. She raved about Tayla's drawings and told her that she was so far ahead of everyone else, not to think twice about it. To just go. Enjoy herself. That the private showing with Guy Cantra wasn't for two weeks.

Tayla was having second and third thoughts, especially since her phone buzzed three times before she even strolled across the parking lot.

Shit. She couldn't do it.

She had to check, but only because she knew that while she was gone, Grace Tandoor was going to take advantage of Tayla's vacation time and use it to put her designs in front of Anna along with making sure she talked as much smack as possible. The worst part was that Tayla knew how Anna worked. It wasn't always about who was the best.

It was about who was willing to kiss her ass the most.

If Anna asked you to go clean the bathroom and you paused and looked at her funny, you'd either be fired or you'd be dressing mannequins for the rest of your career, never seeing a sketch pad again.

Anna had high expectations and the closer you got to her, the more she wanted from you. Everything was a test and it was always pass-fail.

Loyalty was huge to Anna and Tayla made sure that was her middle name.

Tayla should feel confident that five of her evening dresses, three of her casual two-piece mix and match day wear, and one of her men's suits were already selected for the winter line. Tayla's name wouldn't be on them. Anna's would be and Anna would take full credit. But she was okay with that. This was all part of paying her dues.

Or at least that's what she kept telling herself. That this was her last stop. She'd be able to jump off the crazy train and do what she'd set out do when she started down this path.

Build her own line. Her own label. Be her own brand.

She adjusted her sunglasses, pushing them to the top of her head. Holding her cell in her hands, she tapped on the text messages from the only person she'd consider a friend at Anna Declay Designs.

Matthew: *OMG. Girl. Grace had the f'ing nerve to sew her own piece and put it on a mannequin. Anna was not impressed with the design, was not inspired by Grace's balls, but she did take a picture, which means she secretly liked it. That's not good. The last time she liked something like that was when she pulled Renee out of obscurity and even though she fired that one, she used her designs.*

This was exactly what Tayla was worried about. Had Grace tried that while she was still there, Anna might have fired Grace on the spot and not have even noticed because Tayla was the current *it* girl. Anna was all about Tayla and everyone knew how it worked.

Don't upstage Anna's favorite because if you do, you're done. Unless you do it after the favorite screwed up.

Or the favorite child is out of sight, out of mind.

Shit.

Tayla: *Don't tell anyone, but I will be in the office on Monday. Let's see what kind of games Grace wants to play when I'm there.*

Bubbles immediately appeared.

Matthew: *I've got your back, girl. Don't you worry. Enjoy your family and take more than the weekend. Show Grace you're not scared of her. Besides, if she does anything like that again, she will get fired. Anna shamed her in front of everyone. You're good. Just wanted you to know.*

Tayla: *It's Grace we're talking about. She's not stupid. She'll become the yes girl. All she wanted was to get noticed. That's what she did. You watch. She'll be quiet. She'll sit in the front during meetings. She'll offer to get coffee. Dry cleaning. Whatever Anna needs to get back in her good graces.*

Matthew: *Shit. I hadn't thought about it like that. Damn, girl. Your mind works in mysterious ways.*

Tayla: *I'm not taking this whole vacation. Keep me posted.*

She dropped her cell back in her purse and squared her shoulders, mentally preparing herself for her family. She loved them dearly and in many ways, looked forward to spending the weekend with her sisters. They hadn't had a good slumber party in five years.

The moment she stepped into the corner store, part of the tension building in her neck subsided as all the feels of her childhood came crashing down.

The smell of cinnamon and freshly baked bread mixed with pine filled her senses. She closed her eyes and let her favorite memory roll into her mind like an old-fashioned movie.

She and her sisters picking their favorite candies for movie night had always been one of her fondest things from childhood. Her grandfather would set up the projector against the side of the house and they'd snuggle in their sleeping bags, determined to stay awake for the double feature.

It never happened, but they tried.

"Excuse me," a deep, sultry voice said, jerking her into the present.

She blinked, glancing over her shoulder and stepping to the side. "I'm so sorry." She stared into the dark-chocolate eyes of a sexy stranger. They reminded her of hiking through the rich forest at dusk. Her heartbeat lurched to her throat, making it difficult to swallow. She worked with models day in and day out. Gorgeous men and women. Many were eccentric. Others she could describe as unique.

Male models came in all shapes and sizes. It depended on the clothing line. The designer's vision. Some were tall and thin. Others were thick and looked as though they should be a bodyguard.

She let her gaze roll over the stranger's muscles as she thought for a hot minute what in her collection would hang on his body like a second skin. At approximately six one, she guessed him to be about two hundred and twenty pounds of solid mass, but not overstated. He wouldn't bulge through a suit. Actually, she suspected he'd dress up a suit real nice.

"No worries. The smell of this place gets me every time. It's like walking into my grandma's kitchen."

"For me it's like taking a ride into the past." Her eyes soaked in his manliness. It was like he strolled right off the pages of *Fisherman Weekly* with his five-o'clock shadow, dark T-shirt, and jeans that fit loosely on his hips. His feet sported a pair of light-blue boat shoes. She really couldn't tell too much about his hair, except it was dark in color as it peeked out from under his baseball cap and curled at his neck.

He was the kind of man who could flip easily from one look to the other.

She liked that.

But what she really needed to do was stop gawking and start shopping. Her mother gave her one job with two instructions.

Stop at the corner store, pick up the to-go order, and whatever she did, Tayla was not to be late for supper.

When it came to all things family—Tayla was known for being the last one to arrive. Her parents called her the caboose. Tonya thought it hilarious, but she had a horrible habit of being excessively early for everything.

That was just as annoying.

"Wait a minute. You're Tobias and Tessa Johnson's daughter, aren't you?" The man waved his finger. "You're Tayla."

"In the flesh." She shouldn't be surprised that someone shopping at the corner store knew her family. Her great-grandfather had first built a small house on the lake and property had been passed down from generation to generation.

"I've heard a lot about you." He held out his hand. "I'm Gael Waylan. I bought the place next to your parents' house."

Holy cow.

The new neighbor.

The one who had lost his sister and parents in a plane crash. Her parents had told her about him and his tragic story. It broke her heart to hear what had happened to his sister, leaving behind two small children.

However, standing there, staring at him reminded her that she was indeed a woman with a pulse who hadn't had sex in months.

If Tayla were out at a bar and she saw this tall drink of something, she'd certainly consider making a move. Just because she didn't do relationships that lasted very long—or were meaningful in any way—didn't mean she didn't like to let her hair down.

However, she had a couple of rules.

The first one being the most important.

She never dated or fooled around with anyone from her hometown or who knew anyone in her family.

That was risky business.

"It's nice to meet you." When she took his hand, she noticed they were soft, though they did have a few calluses, but she could tell by the texture—and his clean nails—that getting a manicure wasn't beneath his rough exterior.

"I heard you're not only home for the family reunion this weekend, but that you took a vacation."

Her parents had wanted to fix her up a dozen times with different men. She better brace herself for impact. She could see her parents trying to fix her up with this one.

A different time, a different place, she might be interested. But not now. Not at this juncture in her life.

Shit.

This was what happened when she didn't call home regularly—a bone of contention with all her family, but mostly her parents. She texted weekly. More like three times a week.

But she was busy. Her career was demanding, especially now. Anna Declay Designs was expanding. Anna was looking for something new. Something fresh.

And something she could co-design.

Anna had actually said that out loud where people heard it.

What was funny about that concept was almost all of Anna's clothing lines were conceptualized by her employees. Anna didn't do the work. Not anymore.

It had been two years since Anna had an idea of her own and there were rumors she'd never had an original idea in her life. That everything had been built off others.

Tayla ignored the gossip. Her first mentor had told her to keep her head down and do the grunt work and eventually hard work and talent would pay off. So far, that philosophy was working. The only negative had been the promise she'd made to her folks when she missed a family gathering last summer.

To Tayla, it was no big deal. She did her best to keep up relationships. She texted on a regular basis; however, her mother reminded her that words on a tiny screen was not the best form of communication. So, Tayla did her best to video call her mom at least once a week.

That was the best she could do. For now. It would all change when she had her own line.

"A short one," she said.

"Oh. Your dad told me that he had you for two whole weeks."

She tucked her hair behind her ears. She hated the way her parents were always telling random people what she was up to. She understood they were only making small talk.

And they were quite proud of all their girls.

But that didn't change how it made her cringe.

"That had been the original plan, but there's a lot going on at work and I need to get back on Monday." She lifted her finger to her lips. "Please don't tell them. I know how disappointing it will be, but my boss can be demanding and if I don't—sorry. You don't need to hear all this." She jerked her thumb over her shoulder. "Besides. I know my order is ready and if I don't hurry, I'm going to have to listen to a lecture from my mom."

"I totally get it," Gael said. "I look forward to seeing you at dinner tonight."

"Excuse me? What?" She lowered her chin. Shit. It was happening. Her parents were up to their tricks. Not so subtle this time.

"Your parents invited me over for dinner." He cocked his head. "They didn't tell you?"

They might have. She hadn't paid much attention to text messages in the last three days, busy making sure everything at work had been taken care of. She couldn't afford to leave anything to chance.

The vultures were circling, and Tayla had to protect what she'd carved out so far.

"They left that part out," she said without much conviction, but it was all starting to click as to why it was so important she arrive on Thursday night.

The reunion wasn't until Saturday, though some people were coming in Friday night.

At first, she'd thought her parents were worried she wouldn't show.

That was a thing. It had happened before. She wasn't proud of it, but her life was busy. Things came up at work and ever since she'd started working for Anna, Tayla's life was even less her own. If Anna said jump, the response wasn't how high. It wasn't even to lift her feet off the ground. It was to tie rope from her waist and fall from a bridge and hope she didn't go splat on the pavement.

"No offense, but I hadn't planned on having to be on my best behavior tonight. Much less needing to be dressed and be anything other than a drunken fool with my sisters."

He chuckled. "I can always have something come up if that will help you out."

"No. I'm sure my mom's got this whole thing planned and besides my sister's boyfriend will be there and my dad could use another dude outside of Josh to talk to. They have nothing in common."

"Your father doesn't like Josh?"

"You know him?" Why did she always go put her foot in her mouth?

"I've met him once or twice, but I wouldn't go as far as to say I know him, and I can see how maybe he's different."

"That's one way of putting it," she said. "Please keep this between us. Tiki loves him, though I can't honestly see the attraction in any capacity, but if she's happy, then so am I." If Tayla expected her family to understand and respect her life choices, she needed to do the same for everyone else. That meant accepting Josh.

Even if she thought he was a scum-sucking bottom-feeder.

"Not my place to say anything." Gael nodded. "I need to get some ice cream for my nephews. They will be at my house in about forty minutes and if I don't have any, I will lose my status as the best uncle."

"I'll see you tonight."

Gael made his way across the store.

Tayla inwardly groaned. He was certainly something to look at. He might be a nice visual distraction to keep her from pulling out her cell and checking email.

"Hey, Tayla."

She waved to Petey, the store owner who brought out two large bags.

"Your dad already took care of the bill and said if you were going to buy anything—like some gummy fish, which I already put in the bag—to add it to his tab. I'm to argue with you if you try to pay," Petey said as he pulled her in for a big bear hug. "And there are a couple of chocolate chip muffins in there too."

Petey had been a part of her life for as long as she could remember. When she'd been a little girl, he'd set aside her favorite muffin on Sundays. Never once did she have to go without.

"Thanks, Petey. I really appreciate it."

"It's good to see you back in these parts." Petey held her by the biceps. "Has some handsome city slicker taken your heart yet?"

"I told you. I'm don't have time for romance. Not until I have my clothing line."

The sound of an old-fashioned cash register opening caught her attention. She glanced over her shoulder and smiled. Gael paid for his treats and gave her a head nod as he headed out the door.

"Oh, sweetheart." Petey shook his head. "I know your career is important, but don't close your heart. It will harden you in ways you might not be able to recover from."

She knew Petey meant well. He was like a third grandpa, and she valued his kind words.

But she'd set out to create a line with her name on it and she wasn't going to quit.

Her dad didn't raise her to walk away from something she started. She had to finish. She had to know she could do it. Besides, she was stuck between a rock and a hard place. Quitting now would destroy any chance of branching out on her own.

She had to see this through.

Rising up on tiptoe, she kissed Petey's cheek. "Thanks. I'll keep that in mind." No point in arguing with a sweet old man. "Are you still kayaking in the morning?"

"As long as it's not rough or raining, you bet."

"I'll see you out there." She grabbed her bags, turned, and headed out to her vehicle.

Time to face the family.

2

Tayla stared out her childhood window while her sister Tonya's eyes burned a hole in her back. The moment Tayla stepped foot in her parents' house, the judgment began. Instead of engaging, she apologized and went straight to her room to unpack and get ready for dinner, since people other than immediate family were coming.

Tiki had left. She passed her on Cleverdale. She waved and Tiki honked but didn't even slow down. Just kept on driving. Now that Tiki was back, she hadn't bothered to come upstairs and say hello.

She was that pissed.

"The new dock looks great." Tayla decided small

talk might ease some of the tension between her and her sister.

Something she didn't like and needed to figure out how to diffuse. Tonya and Tiki were part of the reason she decided she needed to take the time off. Her family was important.

More important than her career.

She did want to show them that she cared. However, she couldn't lose this opportunity either. She was going to make herself crazy for the next two weeks.

"Dad put that in last year," Tonya said.

Tayla sighed. A lot had changed since she'd been a little girl. Her grandfather had broken down the original parcel of land his father had purchased on Heron Hallow into three lots. His plan had been to have his two boys live next to him. Unfortunately, her uncle passed away when she'd been a baby.

Her grandpa sold the house that Gael lived in at the begging of her grandma who couldn't stand to look at it anymore. It was sold to a rich family who barely used the place until this past winter.

She blinked. All the girls had been on the second floor and had a view of the lake. Her bedroom was on the north side of the house, and her eyes were soaking in a very handsome Gael while he fished on the dock with two young boys.

She remembered he mentioned something about his nephews. She wondered how long Tiki would wait to have kids. Between her two sisters, Tayla always thought Tonya, the baby, would have kids first. Not only was Tonya a wedding planner, but she was a hopeless romantic.

But she was in love with a broken man who wasn't about to give her the time of day.

Tayla's cell buzzed and rattled on the desk. She lifted it and frowned.

An email from Anna.

"Who else is going to be at dinner?" Tayla turned her gaze to her sister. She wanted confirmation about Gael because her parents hadn't owned up to it when Tayla asked. Nope. Her mom gave her the *just family and Josh* response. Her dad responded with *you'd have to ask your mother that question.*

All that meant was her parents were up to something.

"The three of us. Josh. Mom and Dad. Grandpa and Gael," Tonya said from her perch on the bed. She leaned against the headboard, hugging one of the pillows, picking at the fringe on the sides. "They invited Foster, but he said he's got a prior engagement. Mom kept the invite open, but Foster won't come. His ex-wife hasn't been seen in a couple of weeks, so he's worried and he's looking for her in his free time. I did talk him into asking Doug Tanner for help. He spent some time homeless in the area years ago. He might be able to help. Plus, his wife is a retired state trooper and now a private investigator. I'm glad he asked for help, but I also wish he would let that part of his life go. He's not responsible for her anymore. Or at least stop and have dinner."

Tayla opened her mouth to interrupt to get more intel about Gael but couldn't get in a word. Sometimes Tonya spoke faster than a speeding bullet.

"And Dad's been acting weird all day about tonight and for Mom to order half of dinner from the corner store instead of cooking, that's strange, which leads me to believe something else is up."

"Is Josh going to propose?" Tayla asked. "I know Tiki has mentioned they talked about it, but every time she calls me, I feel like she's picking a fight."

"She does that with me too and you didn't hear this from me, but I think Tiki and Josh are having problems."

"Really?" Tayla rested her hands in her lap, but she kept the screen active. Her heart raced while she tried to keep her focus on her family, even though a million thoughts filled her mind about what and why Anna was emailing her on her first day of her vacation. "Why would you say that?"

"Tiki's been distant with me. Actually avoiding me and we live around the corner from each other. She asked Mom to cancel tonight. Literally cancel the entire night. She wanted to do just us girls or nothing. Which isn't unheard of for the three of us, but it is for her to ask. I'm not supposed to know, but Mom refused. I think more so because of Gael and wanting to introduce you to him."

"I already met him at the corner store," Tayla said.

"What did you think of him?"

Tayla wasn't going to answer that question. "Mom needs to stop trying to fix us up. It's gross." She stole a second glance out the window. Gael stood at the edge of the dock. He helped the younger of the two boys cast out his line.

Her body immediately let her know her attraction for Gael was real. Inwardly, she groaned. The longer she looked at him, the more she forgot about work.

In part, that was the point in coming here. That's what a vacation was supposed to be. However, Anna Declay's right-hand girl couldn't afford to take a vacation. Not if she wanted to keep her position in the fashion world.

Tayla eased into the chair and tapped the email icon. Her chest felt heavy as if an elephant were sitting right on the center of it and had no intention of getting up. She was trapped.

The second Anna Declay put Tayla's dress on a celebrity and told the world she was mentoring a designer—creating a new line with that designer—was the moment Tayla had only one choice to achieve her goal.

"I can't imagine you'd find spending an evening with Gael inconvenient. He's hot. And he seems like a really nice guy."

"I can't deny either one," Tayla said. "But Mom forgets I live in New York City. That's a four-hour drive. And why she keeps trying to hook you and Foster up is beyond me. He might be single, but he's not available and you're not going for it. So what's the point in letting her keep trying to set the two of you up?"

Tonya tossed the pillow to the side and criss-crossed her legs. "Why do you have to always do that?"

"Do what?" Tayla peered over her phone. She decided Anna's email could wait a few more minutes. If Anna really had a problem, or there was an issue that required Tayla, or even if Anna wanted to chew her out, she'd call. And keep calling until Tayla picked up.

That's how Anna operated. She didn't quit until she accomplished whatever task she set out to deal with at that moment. That's how Tayla was too. It's one of the reasons Tayla profiled Anna Declay Designs when she'd been working at Harraha. She understood the risks and she was willing to take them.

"Act as if the answer to everything is so simple. Or black and white." Tonya jumped from the bed and made her way across the room.

"Because sometimes it is," Tayla said. "I'm not trying to be mean when it comes to Foster. I know you care about him, and I get you're friends. But he's been through a lot." She'd been saying the same thing to her sister for what seemed like years. "There are some things people don't come back from."

"I'm well aware of what happened and that's not why he was invited tonight. Mom and Dad wanted a reason—other than you—to invite Gael and give him someone to talk to that he might be able to relate to. He lost his sister and parents recently and they feel bad for him. Not to mention they want to make Josh feel comfortable, which makes me batshit crazy. Why we bend over backward to make his awkward ass fit in is beyond me. If he's going to be a member of this family, he needs to figure it out. And he needs to stop acting like you and I are the enemy."

"Something we agree on."

"I doubt that. I equate him with your career."

"That hurt," Tayla said, staring at her sister. "I'm here, aren't I? I'm making an effort, aren't I? What more do you want?"

"I want for this antagonistic bullshit to stop." Tonya waved her finger between her and Tayla. "I'm so tired of you and I having these same fights. These same discussions. I love you and I want to laugh with you like we used to, but you don't have time for us anymore."

"We all have jobs. Lives. That's what happens when people grow up."

"Oh, please," Tonya said. "I'm not asking for you to come home every weekend. All I'm saying is that work has consumed you and you can't see it."

Actually, Tayla did see it, but she wasn't prepared to acknowledge it to her family. Not even her sisters. She knew she'd get to the point where she'd have more time. That day would come. Tayla tapped her screen. Her heart rate continued to increase. She needed to find a way to end the conversation with her sister. She didn't want to argue. "We should probably get downstairs. Why don't you go, and I'll follow—"

"I'm not going without you."

Tayla glared.

"You're going to read an email or whatever that is on your phone and you're going to get caught up in work. Then you'll be late to dinner, breaking your promise to Mom. What a great way to start the weekend."

"I told you that I would have to check on things while I'm gone. Come on, Tonya. There are designers at work who would toss their children under the bus to be where I am right now. And with me gone, they will do whatever it takes to get Anna's attention. One person already has."

"You give that woman too much power," Tonya muttered.

"It's important and will only take a second."

"Well, too late for that now. Josh just pulled in and Tiki is already out the front door." Tonya leaned against the windowsill. "Come on. Put it away. It's family time."

"It will only take a few minutes for me to read it."

Tayla shook her head with her finger hovering over Anna's name. The subject line read: *Details for New Line.*

Tayla couldn't fuck this up. Her entire career rested on this opportunity.

"Everything is finally coming together. Go downstairs. I'll join you shortly."

"Don't you dare leave early." Tonya tapped her finger on the wood desk. "You're going to hit the road on Monday, aren't you?"

"That all depends on this email," Tayla admitted. "Look. I promised Mom and Dad I'd be home for the reunion, which I know is hard for Grandpa to have all of Mom's side of the family here, but everyone needs to understand how important this is to me."

"You're miserable." Tonya let out a long breath. "Every time I talk to you, you're on edge. Moody. I get you want your own line, but there are other ways to do that besides sucking up to a woman who is using you and your creative work. Everything you told me about this Anna person isn't good. According to you, she's never publicly given to anyone. Every time someone—"

"I don't need a lecture about my boss and her business practices." Tayla gritted her teeth. Her baby sister was right. She had friends who had done Kickstarter campaigns and had small local shops that featured their own creations.

They were still living the dream.

Just not at the Anna Declay Designs level.

And so what if Anna was using Tayla. That's how it worked. Anna was a world-famous designer who used a number of understudies. Only a select few would be showcased.

"You need something because we're all tired of the way you've been acting lately. I want my sister back."

"I admit I've been under a lot of pressure. But this is it. This is my big break." She waved her cell. "I've worked too hard to let an opportunity like this slip through my fingers. I'm on the verge. It's happening. I've got a private showing that I'm doing my own designs for. If this guy likes them, Anna plans on putting my name on them."

"And then what's next?" Tonya asked. "I mean, when does it end? When do you get to slow down and smell some roses?" Tonya held up her hand. "I don't mean to sound like Mom and Dad. But the last few times we've visited, you were stressed out and when something good does happen to you, in all honesty you don't seem happy about it because you've already moved on to the next thing that this

Anna woman needs you to do. And you even said so yourself that she doesn't always come through. That she's screwed over a bunch of other designers before you."

"She has. I understand and trust me, I'm being careful and protecting myself. But she's never gone this far with anyone else. There's never even been a hint of a private showing before me."

"That you know of," Tonya said. "You need to take a breath and look at yourself in the mirror. You're not the same person you were even six months ago."

She was so sick and tired of defending her career choices. "Once I get my own line, I can make different decisions. Have more choices with how I live my life. I have to pay my dues." She tapped her cell. "I do really need to look at this."

"All right. But if you're not downstairs in twenty, I'm sending Josh up here to get you."

Tayla groaned. "Don't you dare."

"Okay. I'll send Gael."

Before Tayla could respond, her little sister was out the door. Shit. Knowing Tonya, she'd absolutely send Gael.

She opened the email and prepared for the worst.

Hey, Tayla,

Hope you're enjoying Lake George. I think I need to buy a summer retreat or something. But I digress.

Ugh. She sounded exactly the same in email as she did in person, and it was as annoying in the written word as it was when having a conversation. As a designer, Anna was the best. She was sheik. Overstated. Priceless. She had the attitude. And everyone wanted to be her.

Including Tayla.

She was thirsty for Anna's attention and right now she was drunk on it, but she could do without Anna's crazy personality.

Especially now that she was back in the most peaceful spot in the world.

Unfortunately, I have a little bad news for you. We need to move up the private showing for Guy Contra and I will need your designs next week. Friday at the latest. I know you're always so on top of things, so I figure you can finish them up and send them to me. If there is a problem, I'll let you know, but I doubt it. I loved the direction you were going, and I know Guy Contra will too. I'm so excited for you.

Anna

Shit.

Double shit.

If Anna wanted them Friday, that meant she better send them in no later than Thursday.

Better yet, hand them to her in the office.

She could go to the city for two days and come back next weekend. That would be fine. She'd make her family understand. She would sit them down. Have a good old family-style meeting like they used to when she was in high school and needed to discuss something important with her parents. All she had to do was calmly explain the situation and promise she'd be back.

Hell, she'd show her parents that by leaving her suitcase and some of her belongings behind so that she'd have no choice but to return.

The designs were mostly done. They needed tweaks. And it would be easier for her to work on them here, where she had a clear mind away from the stress of the office. She'd planned on doing it this way because she couldn't risk Grace seeing any of them since she had stolen ideas in the past.

Tayla wasn't about to let that happen.

Not when her entire career was on the line.

Okay. She would stay until Wednesday. Maybe Thursday morning. Finish the designs and head back to the city where she and Matthew could put together a presentation and make a splash of it.

Phew.

This was happening.

Her career was about to take off.

Soon, everyone in the fashion world would know who Tayla Johnson was and they'd want her designs on their rack.

Celebrities would be calling her to create a one-of-a-kind red-carpet outfit for all their social events.

Her fingers shook as she typed her response.

Matthew had his doubts about how far Tayla had been willing to go down this rabbit hole, but it was going to pay off.

It had to.

GAEL WAYLAN CAST the line out into the water before handing it to his young nephew.

"Thanks," Sam said. He plopped himself down in his little folding chair and wiggled his feet back and forth. He'd last maybe five minutes before he'd grow impatient.

That was unless, of course, a fish got caught on the line.

"Daddy!" Benny called as he raced across the dock toward the house.

"Hey, buddy." Greg scooped up his six-year-old son and hugged him tight.

"I don't want to go home." Sam dropped his pole to the dock and folded his chubby little arms in defiance.

It took all of Gael's energy not to laugh.

"If it's okay with your uncle Gael, you can fish for a half hour before we take off. But then we have to go home and pack to go visit Grandma and Grandpa Hannah."

"Can we, Uncle Gael? Can we stay for a bit?" Sam stared up at him.

"That's absolutely fine with me." He ruffled Sam's hair.

"Cool." Sam went back to staring at the bobber in the water.

Benny raced back to his pole and dropped to his perch on the dock.

"There's beer in the cooler if you'd like one," Gael said.

"Is there water in there too?"

Gael nodded as he strolled to the end of the dock and took a seat. He adjusted his baseball cap and stretched out his legs.

"How were the boys today?"

"Perfect angels."

Greg laughed. "Wish I could say they were like that for me every day."

"They aren't my kids."

"I can't thank you enough for taking them today. These teacher conference days kill me with daycare."

"Until I figure out my work situation, you can ask me to watch them anytime. I can also come down to you. No problem."

"I appreciate that," Greg said.

"Sam doesn't want you to know, but he did have an accident. I washed his clothes."

"Did something trigger him?" Greg's job as a psychiatrist often has him talking in terms that Gael didn't understand or that he thought didn't make sense when it came to children. Especially when it was Greg's own kids.

But what did Gael know. He wasn't a father.

"If you mean did something upset him, sort of." Gael ran a hand over his face. "We went for a walk and there was a lady down the street walking her dog with her daughter. I believe it made him think of his mom. He didn't make it home and he didn't ask to use the bushes. I didn't notice the dance until it was too late."

"Seeing kids with their moms still gets to both of

them. They don't always know how to verbalize their emotions."

"I hope I did the right thing by not making a big deal about it. I told him that it happens to a lot of boys, and we went swimming while we waited for his clothes to be cleaned."

"That's the best way to handle it. And to remind him to listen to his body. When he's got to go, he's got to tell an adult." Greg leaned back and let out a long breath. "Everyone says kids are resilient. I think that's a true statement, but I also believe in some ways, this is harder for them than it for us. They don't have the same coping skills we do and it's not like we can teach them. They don't have emotional maturity. They don't have the ability to understand the way we do."

"I don't understand," Gael said. Sometimes his brother-in-law got a little weird. "I couldn't explain to them what happened or why if I had to." He faced Greg. "Does death ever make sense?"

"Yes and no," Greg said. "It's a part of life. The normal progression is we get old, we die. That's what's supposed to happen in a perfect world. But that doesn't happen most of the time. Tragic deaths happen every day and our society—"

"Greg. Stop." Gael sometimes couldn't handle

the words that came out of Greg's mouth. "I can't believe I'm going to be the one to say this, but you're not at work anymore."

Greg laughed. "Sorry. I gave an all-day workshop today. One of the topics was depression and grief and how differently it affects people." He dropped his head back and rubbed his temple. "I had to force myself into this monotone emotionless state. I'm kind of still there. Otherwise, I would have broken down in the middle of it and cried like a baby."

"Like you always tell me—you're in a safe space here."

"I'm still getting used to the idea that I like you." Greg had a dry sense of humor, something that Gael hadn't known about him before Piper had died.

There were a lot of things Gael hadn't known because he'd been too busy becoming a selfish prick to spend time with the people who mattered the most.

His family.

It took his sister and parents dying for Gael to wake up and see the kind of man he'd become.

And he didn't like that person.

"I had been avoiding doing those lectures at all," Greg started. "I've always enjoyed teaching as well as seeing patients, but since Piper died, it's been hard because of the topics I cover."

"I can only imagine." Gael couldn't fathom being a doctor, much less a psychiatrist and one who worked in emergency medicine. Greg was a do-gooder. The kind of man who wanted to change the world. He wanted to make it a better place for the next generation.

He said it all started with mental wellness.

Gael was beginning to believe he had a valid point.

"Piper would have been proud of me today, though. I made it through, and I agreed to teach a seminar next semester at the college. It's only a lecture so it's not an actual class. But still. I'm living and I know that's what Piper would want."

"Uncle Gael. My bobber's gone," Sam said. "I can't see it anymore."

"It's not gone." Gael jumped to his feet and jogged down the wood dock. "You got a fish on your line." He stood behind his nephew, helping him to his feet. "Crank slowly." He glanced over his shoulder. "Greg. The net is by the cooler. Can you grab it?"

Greg nodded.

"The fish is getting away," Sam said as the bobber popped out of the water and then disappeared again. The line pulled tight, and the pole bent over.

"No, it's not. It's just swimming and trying to take us with him." Gael didn't know much about fishing. What he had learned came from magazines, YouTube videos, and Maxwell Johnson, Tayla's grandfather. But he didn't need to be a great fisherman to know that whatever was on the other end of this line was bigger than the sunfish they'd been catching and throwing back most of the day. He gripped the pole over Sam's hands and gave it a little tug.

Damn.

He worried if he wasn't standing there and Sam gripped tightly, that fish was going to drag Sam right into the water.

"Sam. Can I help you reel this in?"

"Sure," the little boy said.

Gael placed his hand over Sam's and together they began to bring this bad boy in.

"Where do you want me?" Greg asked as he stood next to his son. "Oh. Wow. Look." He pointed. "It's going to jump."

The line shifted as the fish tried to swim away, tugging at the pole. The line slacked at the surface and a largemouth bass flew out of the water as if it were a rocket ship launching toward the stars.

"Wow." Benny was on his feet, standing behind his little brother. "Did you see that? It has to be at least ten or eleven inches long."

"I sure did, son," Greg said. "And I agree. It's a big one."

"If it were bass season, it might even be a keeper." Gael wished it were the middle of June and not the end May. "Let's keep cranking at a steady pace." He did his best to make Sam feel as though he was the one in control, even though Gael gripped Sam's hand tightly.

"Here, Benny." Greg handed the net to his older boy. "Why don't you and I kneel down and get ready to help bring this fish home, but remember, we're going to have to let him go."

"We know, Dad. We've been doing this all day," Benny said.

"Get ready." Gael shifted the pole to the right, keeping the fish from swimming under the dock. "Sam and I are going to bring it close. Once it's at the surface you need to—"

"See it, Dad?" Benny said with excitement laced in every syllable. "Now, Dad!"

"We got it." Sam jumped up and down, his arms

flapping wildly as if he were a bird trying to take flight. "He's huge!" Gael grabbed him by the biceps before he tumbled into the cold waters below. The wood below his foot shook. He glanced up as Maxwell came limping down the dock.

"That's a nice fish." Maxwell held up a measuring tape. "Just for curiosity, let's see how big it is." He held up the tape to the fish Sam tried to hold but could barely manage with his fat little fingers.

The fish wiggled and fought to be free.

"Would you look at that," Maxwell said with a smile. "It's almost twelve inches long. Hopefully you boys can recatch this bad boy in a few weeks."

"We better toss him back in," Gael said.

Sam nodded. He squeezed it with both hands and grunted as he heaved it back into the water.

It flopped on its side, disappearing into the crystal-blue waters of Lake George.

"Well, that was exciting," Maxwell said. "No one's caught a fish that size off these docks in a few years. You boys are lucky."

Gael ruffled both boys' heads.

"Unfortunately, it's time for me to take them home," Greg said. "Let's go up to the house and get our stuff."

"Everything is in the family room in their backpacks. All packed up and ready to go," Gael said. He knelt down and hugged both his nephews. "I love you guys. You be good for your grandparents, and I'll see you soon. Okay?"

"Love you too," they said in unison before taking off like a bat out of hell toward the house.

"Thanks again. I'll see you this weekend?" Greg asked. "While it will be nice to have some alone time, it will be weird not to be with the boys twenty-four seven."

"Absolutely." Gael nodded. He watched Greg run off after his boys.

"They have a ton of energy," Maxwell said. "I remember when the girls were little. I used to ask their parents where the off switch was."

"That's funny." Gael clutched his chest. Every single time those two boys left, he had sharp pains rip through his heart. He imagined that's what it would feel like if he'd been shot.

"They are exhausting, and I often need a nap after a day with them," Gael said.

"You are still coming to dinner tonight, aren't you?" Maxwell asked.

Ever since meeting Tayla at the corner store, Gael had contemplated changing his mind.

But that would be rude, and Piper would have

something to say about that if he did. One of the things he'd been working on was listening to that inner voice—which was always his little sister's voice—being his moral compass.

However, in this case he wasn't so sure going to dinner was the right thing. When he thought about who all was invited, he realized he was being set up.

Literally.

And he wasn't sure how he felt about that except for one thing.

He had an instant attraction to Tayla. It wasn't all the things he'd been told about her or even the fact she was smoking hot.

It was simply her.

She had an ease with the way she carried herself. The way she communicated. It was natural. Not forced. Confident, but with a hint of insecurity. Not too much, but just enough to make him want to know more.

And that scared the shit out of him.

"I wouldn't miss it for the world," Gael said. Not going would be inconsiderate to the entire Johnson family. It had nothing to do with the woman staring at him from her bedroom window.

3

"Tessa, dinner was fabulous. I can't thank you enough for including me." Gael placed his napkin on his plate and leaned back in his chair. He glanced around the table.

All three sisters home.

The three musketeers together again.

For the last month or so, every time he ran into Tessa or Tobias, all they could talk about was the fact they'd have all three kids under one roof and how much that meant to them.

If Gael's heart could break again, it would. He knew his parents wanted their family together and he was too busy becoming somebody to spend time with the people in his life who matter most.

And now they were gone.

He couldn't make up for lost time, but he could change how he lived his life going forward.

"Anytime," Tessa said. "I've been meaning to have you over. I just wish I had cooked."

"My mom is the best cook. Better than any fancy chef you'll find downstate," Tayla said with a smile. It was genuine, and so was the compliment, yet there was an underlying tension that had plagued the dinner and it wasn't just the issues with Tayla and her job. Gael sensed conflict between Tiki and her boyfriend.

He couldn't explain it, since being sensitive to others' emotions was a new concept to him, but something in the way they interacted compared to other couples made him think not everything was coming up roses. It was the little things like every time Josh took her hand, she held it for a second and then pulled away, as if she thought better of it.

Outside of that, Gael had to admit, he enjoyed the family dynamics. The sisters had fallen into this cute banter and had a few inside jokes that he hadn't a clue as to what they meant, but he loved listening to them laugh.

It reminded him of Piper.

He struggled to remember what she sounded

like, but when he found that pitch, it was music to his ears.

"That's sweet of you to say, sweetheart, but you haven't been home in the last few years long enough to enjoy it." Tessa stood, taking a couple of the plates. "And you missed half this meal because you were *handling* something for work."

"Mom. That's not fair," Tayla said behind a tight jaw. She glanced in his direction. Her eyes were a dark, deep blue and they conveyed what most would confuse with drive and determination.

But in reality, what lurked behind those intense orbs was fear. The only question he had was of what?

He knew when he was chasing dollar signs he believed he was living the dream. He understood that in order to stay on top, he needed to work harder. Work more. Work better. He was one bad deal away from falling back down to the bottom.

And each new deal was the one that was going to take him to the next level.

There was always going to be bigger and more and if he closed his eyes for even a second, it would all be gone. His career would be over. He'd be just another advisor with average clients making an okay living.

That wasn't an option. He thought that would be worse than anything.

Only, he never imagined what it would be like if anyone removed his family. It didn't matter that he didn't see them and barely spoke to them. They were still there. In the peripheral. He knew he could see them or talk to them if he wanted to.

His ex-wife warned him when she left that he was going to regret his life choices one day. That she wasn't the only thing he was going to lose.

Part of him believed she'd come back. That she wasn't serious. That she loved the lifestyle that he provided too much.

Part of him couldn't have cared less what she did because he was a selfish prick who cared more about money and power than people. He told himself that either she wanted him or she didn't, and if it was the latter—her loss. The truly sad part was he'd been so wrapped up in the thirst for climbing the financial ladder he hadn't comprehended what *he'd* lost. Not even when he climbed into bed at night with a glass of wine and forced sleep to come so he could wake up and start his day filled a hunger that couldn't ever be satisfied.

However, the true tragedy had been the fact he didn't understand death was permanent and when his parents and sister were killed, that was it. They were gone. There were no do-overs. No second chances. No tomorrows.

"Sweetheart," Tobias said. "It's not fair that we were all waiting for you, especially our guests."

Tayla opened her mouth, but her father held up his hand.

"I don't want to argue, and I do understand your career is important to you. I remember those days and I'm proud of you and what you're accomplishing. But we don't get to see you very often and it's not too much to ask that you give us your full attention for a few hours."

Gael recoiled in his chair. On the one hand, he wanted to wrap a protective arm around Tayla. There was nothing worse than being a grown adult and having your parent lecture you like a child.

He'd been there before, and it wasn't fun.

However, listening to Tobias' words made him miss his parents and sister even more.

Tayla wiped her mouth with her napkin and rose. "I need to use the ladies' room."

"And then you can help your mother with the dishes." Tobias lowered his chin.

"I'm happy to help," Tayla said with a touch of sarcasm.

"I think I'm going to call it a night," Maxwell, Tayla's grandfather, said. "Tonya, how about you walk me home."

"I'd love to, Grandpa." Tonya rose, helping her granddad to his feet.

"Tiki and Josh. Could you please go start the fire?" Tobias asked.

"Would be happy to." Josh was on his feet in seconds and out the door quicker than a bolt of lightning flashing in the sky.

"I'm sorry about that," Tobias said. "I'm not sure what has gotten into my entire family. It's like we were catapulted back to when they were in middle school."

Gael laughed as memories of him running through the front yard with the hose and spraying down Piper and her best friend filled his mind. "No worries. I'm having a lovely time." The old Gael would have declined the dinner invitation from the Johnson family because it hadn't come from a client or a friend he had benefits with. Seven months ago, Gael had been driven by two things. Money and power.

As a financial advisor to some of the richest people in the country, his job wasn't just to make them more money.

His entire world was centered on making his clients look good.

He found them the right investments and then fed them the proper talking points, so they sounded as if they'd been the one who gave their advisor the tip to buy the stock. Or invest in a start-up.

And Gael had gotten off on it until the dreadful evening when he'd been sitting in a bar having his third old-fashioned and he happened to glance up at the television.

The headlines had sucker punched his gut and changed his perspective forever.

But it wouldn't bring back his parents or his little sister.

Or the fact he'd ignored their calls. Their texts. And the fact that his grandfather was on his death bed, and they were headed to Florida to see him while Greg had stayed behind with their two little boys.

Gael swallowed his last sip of wine. Greg had tried to reach him for two hours before making the painful decision to allow the press to release the names of the souls who had died in the small plane crash.

Tobias reached across the table, lifting the bottle of wine. "You look like you could use a refill."

"I'd love one. Thank you." Gael held out his tumbler while Tobias poured a rich red cabernet.

"Why don't we take this outside?" Tobias nodded his head.

Gael followed Tobias through the newly remolded family room. It had been done in a modern flair but hadn't lost its lake feel with its wood beams across the cathedral ceilings and its nautical decor.

When Gael stepped outside and the cool Adirondack air hit his skin, he was glad he'd worn jeans and a sweatshirt. While it had been unseasonably warm this spring, the weather could change on a dime this time of year.

"What a beautiful night." Gael slipped into one of the big chairs facing the lake. Tiki and Josh sat on the bench by the dock and looked as though they were in an intense conversation.

"This never gets old," Tobias said. "May I ask you a question? A personal one."

"Sure."

"You're a young man. About my Tayla's age. I understand you're grieving, and you can't put a timeline on that. But I was curious if you had any intention on going back to financial advising."

"No," Gael answered quickly. "But if you ever want to talk to me about your investments, feel free."

"Oh. Thanks. I appreciate that." Tobias lifted his glass and swirled his wine. "One of Tessa's brothers is a financial planner. Not of the caliber that you were, but he's done well for us. I was asking because if something were to happen to me and one of my girls gave up everything to help out the rest of the family, I'd worry about how sustainable that would be."

"I did pretty well for myself. I'll be okay financially." Gael tapped the center of his chest. His father would have asked someone that question.

"That would honestly be the least of my concerns." Tobias arched a fatherly brow. "I realize this is none of my business and you're a grown man. I also just had a mini argument with my daughter about the fact she doesn't know how to balance work and family, but the key word there is *balance*. It's important and eventually you're going to need something outside of helping your brother-in-law with his boys, though I'm sure he's grateful to you."

There was more to that story than Gael was willing to tell Tobias.

Or anyone for that matter.

The truth was that he was lucky Greg even let

him spend time with his nephews. Greg had been pissed that Gael hadn't gone with his parents. That all he'd done is buy tickets on a private charter.

He'd blamed Gael for Piper's death.

So did Gael.

"When I quit my job, I said I'd give myself a full year before going back to anything," Gael said. "Seven months out, I know I don't want to go back to the world I left and one thing I'd like to do is invest in a couple of small businesses. I just haven't found the right ones yet."

"That's interesting, but what about you? What do you want?"

Gael's throat tightened. It became difficult to breathe. He wanted for his nephews to have their mother back.

But that could never be.

"I honestly don't know," Gael said. "For as long as I can remember, I've had a knack for numbers, but I'm not sure I have a passion for it anymore."

Tobias made a grunting sound. "Tayla has always been a little fashionista. She's always had an eye for it too. We bought her a sewing machine when she was in the sixth grade and by eighth grade, she was making her own clothes. We thought she was passionate."

"Sounds like she was and still is." Gael understood how a rich, thick drive could get caught in your veins. It moved slowly like a snake slithering through the woods until it found its prey. Then it coiled, waiting for the perfect time to lunge out and strike. He remembered that moment. The opportunity to take one road or the other.

The choice.

But passions that were that palpable often lied, only giving you the illusion of the ability to perhaps go a different direction.

"Not anymore." Tobias sighed, leaning forward. "I know my daughter and she's lost all the reasons she's wanted to become a designer in the first place. I get having her name on a line of clothing has always been the end goal and I don't want her to give up her dream. That's not what I'm saying. But it's the way she's going about it and how she's changed. It's as if she's sold her soul to the devil and the devil isn't even going to live up to his end of the bargain."

Gael was about to ask what that meant exactly, but the sound of the screen door slamming shut caught his attention.

Tayla, followed by her mom and sister Tonya, made their way to the fire pit.

Tessa eased into the chair next to her husband

and Tonya next to her mom. Tayla had made herself comfortable in the chair across from Gael, making it impossible for him to ignore her presence. Not that he would, but now she was in his line of sight. The flames inched toward the stars and the moon dancing in the sky. Her face glowed like a porcelain God in the light from the fire. If anyone had asked Gael to describe what perfection looked like, it would be Tayla.

He cleared his throat and smiled. Since Gael had lost his parents and sister, he'd literally slowed his life to a snail's pace and stopped to smell every single rose. He did his best to enjoy all moments of his day. Every detail mattered. Even the smallest.

He'd given up his expensive loft in the financial district, quit his job, and moved to Lake George to get to know the only family he had left.

It had been a struggle and had taken him this long to get Greg to trust that he wasn't going to run off and leave Benny and Sam heartbroken. Greg had reason to be concerned. Gael had promised to show up at various family gatherings, only to leave the family wondering if he'd run his car into a ditch. It got so bad that Greg threatened to stop inviting him to things. Actually begged Piper to cut him out of their lives.

Now that he'd been able to spend some time alone with his nephews and he and Greg were working on their friendship, Gael had found himself wondering what the next step in his life would be. He was only thirty-eight. He had a lot of living left to do. His sister and parents wouldn't want him to sit around and mourn forever. They would want him to be a positive role model for Benny and Sam.

Balance.

He liked what Tobias had to say and it made sense.

It would be nice to find a second career. Something that maybe would give him an opportunity to settle down. Maybe fall in love.

Have a family of his own.

Give Benny and Sam some cousins.

"Tayla. Did you know Gael used to live in the city?" Tessa asked.

"I believe it was mentioned," Tayla said.

"What part of the city do you live in?" Gael kept his focus on her blue eyes. They were more intense than his on Friday when checks hit his account.

And he remembered how his blood boiled when he watched the stocks go up and his clients went wild.

But none of that lasted. It wasn't real. It wasn't what mattered.

What did were moments with family. The things you couldn't get back.

More money?

He could make that. Hell, if he ran out, he could go get a job at the local grocery store if he had to. But time with family and friends, making memories? That was the real payday.

"In Chelsea," Tayla said.

"I lived in lower Manhattan for years."

"Expensive," Tayla said.

Gael laughed. "You can say that again."

"I think we need another bottle of wine." Tobias stood, holding out his hand. "Tessa, why don't we also bring out a tray of s'mores."

"Oh. That sounds perfect." Tessa jumped to her feet. "Tonya. Why don't you come help?"

"Sure. Whatever." Tonya leaned over and whispered something to Tayla, who shook her head and smiled before catching his gaze. "We'll be back."

Gael rested his hand against his chest, feeling his heart beat. Sometimes feeling his pulse reminded him to be present. He'd missed out on so much because he'd been chasing the wrong dream. Money wasn't what made the world go round.

People were.

"I've been looking forward to the right moment to tell you how sorry I am for your loss," Tayla said. The fire crackled like fireflies racing around as children tried to catch them for their mason jars. "I didn't want to blurt it out across the table."

He stood and moved closer. He didn't feel like yelling across the tall flames. Or at least that's what he told himself, when the reality was he wanted to be closer to Tayla.

Her long dark hair shone under the white glow of the moon. She had a sweet smile when she allowed herself to relax, and that hadn't happened but once or twice during the evening. He noticed she kept her cell close, and she checked it often.

He remembered those days.

"Thanks. I appreciate that."

"I'm sorry if it seems like my family was gossiping. We weren't. However, it was mentioned, and then I saw you with two young children on your dock and you mentioned spending time with—"

"My nephews," he said with a strong sense of pride. "My sister's kids. They are amazing. Benny is six and Sam's four. I adore them and love every second I get to be with them in any capacity."

She lifted her glass of white wine and waved out

in front of her. "I'm sure they love coming to visit you here."

"I hope they do," Gael said. "Greg, my sister's husband, lives in Saratoga Springs. They had talked about buying a summer place, but now with Greg's job at the hospital and taking care of the kids, I don't think he can swing it for a while, so I did it."

"Wow. That's generous."

"This is my home, so it wasn't just for them." When he first bought the house, Greg accused him of doing it out of guilt.

Greg wasn't wrong.

But that hadn't been the only reason.

As kids, Lake George had been a place he and Piper loved to visit. They both went to a summer camp on Pilot Knob Road and his childhood memories were filled with snapshots of camping on the islands. This was one way he could honor his sister and parents.

It helped keep them alive in his heart.

"I don't mean to pry, but what do you do for work now?" Tayla asked.

"Right now, nothing," he admitted. "I'm starting to consider my options and I'm looking for a business to invest in. A creative opportunity. One where my contribution can be running the numbers. Keeping the books. Dealing with all the financials."

"So, not a complete silent partner."

He laughed. "Piper, my sister, once told me that I didn't have a clue as to how to keep my opinions to myself. When she and I lived together in the city while she was still doing art full-time, she'd often ask me my thoughts on a given painting. Whenever my opinions weren't exactly what she wanted to hear, she'd toss a brush at me and tell me to be nicer. Kinder."

"I've learned not to ask my sisters for their thoughts on my designs. Though, half the time it ends with *if that doesn't get picked up by your boss, will you make it for me?*"

"I've seen some of your work. You're quite talented." Being in finance, he had to look his best. All the time. He had to dress like he had old money and new money at the same time. And he had to make sure that he never dressed better than his clients, but close to it. They had to think he was making money, but not more than them. And not certainly off them, though that was the point.

It was a game he got off on and just thinking about it made his heart burst just a little.

Though, not enough that he ever wanted to go

back. Those days were done.

"Thank you. I appreciate you saying that." She turned her head and sighed. "How long have those two been sitting down there like that?"

"Since I got outside."

"Shit," she mumbled. "I was hoping Tonya was wrong about them and I was simply a bitch who didn't see real happiness when it was staring me in the face."

"Whatever's going on with them has been brewing for a while now." Gael should have kept his observations to himself. The first month he'd lived on Herron Hallow, he did his best to be invisible to his neighbors. All he wanted to do was set up a home that Greg would bring the boys to on the weekend, even if only for an afternoon of fishing. Or a day out on the boat.

Gael's only goal had been to get to know his sister's kids.

And Greg.

However, as time passed, he found himself sitting out on his front deck—observing. Watching. Studying. The Johnsons had become both a life lesson and a window into the past.

It warmed his heart to see how a family interacted with each other and supported one another. It might be slightly dysfunctional, but that's what made it rich and loving. No family was perfect. That would be boring and one-dimensional. Sometimes the things he missed the most about Piper were those silly things that brought them conflict. Like how she always tattled on him when they were kids. Or how she'd always managed to get away with everything and he'd get busted every single time.

And yet, his sister, until he'd chosen his career over all else, had his back.

"How do you know that?" Tayla asked.

"I've been around them a couple of times when they've been here on the weekends." He tried to keep it cool, saying very little. He didn't want to come off as a creeper who spied on people. Or someone who butted their nose in where it didn't belong.

Sound carried over water and Tiki and her boyfriend tended to forget that when they were out on the big floaty in front of the docks. It wasn't that Gael was eavesdropping while he fished and enjoyed the scenery; however, it was kind of hard not to when Josh raised his voice or Tiki got emotional.

"What does that mean?" she asked.

He shifted his gaze. The unhappy couple hadn't moved and no one else had returned to the fire pit. He'd opened this can of worms. It wouldn't be fair for him to backpedal now. "It's not that they fight, but there is always this intensity between the two of them that is fueled by negative emotions." No one in Gael's past would describe him as sensitive or an empath.

That was something he'd been working on and the more in tune he'd become with his kinder, softer self.

She polished off the rest of her beverage, setting the glass on the table. "You don't know them and to make that kind of judgment about someone's happiness over a couple interactions is irresponsible. It makes you look like a nosy neighbor and a gossip."

The old Gael would have to prove why he was right, and she was wrong. He'd jump right down her throat and tell her all the specific things he'd seen right along with hitting her where it hurt.

Her weak spot.

Her vulnerability, which was still her family and how she perceived her relationship with them.

She'd yet learned to mask that, and it could destroy her in business if she wasn't careful.

Of course, that might not be a bad thing considering she'd lost any sense of balance, something that Gael worried about himself for when he went back into the workforce.

"I suppose it does make me look that way, but you asked, so I answered. Truthfully."

"But in a generic way," she added, waggling her finger toward Josh and Tiki. "You have no idea what they are discussing."

"You're right. I don't. But does it look like they're enjoying themselves?" The moment he spoke the words, all hell broke loose.

"No. I'm done. We're done. I can't do this anymore," Tiki yelled. She stood and turned.

"Don't walk away from me." Josh grabbed her by the biceps. "I've done everything you've asked. It's time you do this for me."

Gael pressed his hands against the wood armrests, pushing the chair back. He tolerated a lot of things, and this wasn't any of his business.

But he wasn't going to stand there and let a man put his hands on a woman in anger. He drew the line there.

"Are you serious right now?" Tiki said. "You don't get to ask anything of me. Not after what you did. I think it's best you leave. No need to say goodbye. I'll let my family know what happened."

"Tiki. Don't do this," Josh pleaded with both hands holding her firmly in his grasp. "Don't tell your family anything. They already know something's up. If you really want me to leave, I will. But at least let me say thank you and we can talk about this tomorrow."

"Are you willing to go to therapy?" Tiki asked.

"Are you willing to get marri—"

"This is not a negotiation. Either we go to counseling together, and then maybe we can discuss getting married. Or there's nothing left to talk about," Tiki said.

Gael wanted to slink away into the night, but he couldn't. He felt like a fly on the wall.

Or maybe a deer in headlights.

"I don't understand why we can't move forward with—"

"Just go. I'll explain to my parents. It's not like they didn't notice what a jerk you've been tonight."

"Me? You're the one who has been acting like a bitch." Josh had both hands on Tiki and moved closer.

Gael took two steps in their direction.

"What are you doing?" Tayla inched close behind him, resting her hands on his shoulders. Her hot breath tickled his neck.

"I don't like the way he's handling her."

"You and me both. I've never seen him like this," Tayla whispered.

Gael wanted to remind Tayla that was because she hadn't been around much, but it wasn't the time, the place, and he wasn't the person to do it—at least not at this moment.

"Well, I earned that right when you cheated on me," Tiki said.

"Oh shit," Tayla said. "That sucks." Her fingers dug into Gael's sides. "I can't believe he did that to her. What a slime."

"Agreed," Gael said. "If he doesn't take a hike in a minute or two, I'll go make sure he does."

"And I've apologized," Josh said. "I've stopped going to all the places where I could possibly run into her. I let you track my phone. I text you almost the second you message me. You have access to everything. I'm like a man-child and it's not enough for you. I don't know what else to do."

"Leave. That's it. That's all I want. Just leave." Tiki shrugged her shoulders and pointed toward the driveway. "Don't say a word to anyone in my family and let's end this right here. Right now."

"I can't believe you're going to throw away what we have because I made a mistake." Josh took a step back. "While we'd been broken up, I might add."

"Oh, my God. Get the hell out of here. Now. Go."

Josh held up both his hands. "Fine. But you're

going to come crawling back and this time I might not take you back." He stuffed his hands in his pockets and stormed off up the pathway toward his vehicle.

Gael let his muscles relax. He glanced over his shoulder, grateful that Tayla's parents hadn't witnessed that outburst.

Tiki marched in their direction.

"Oh, sweetie. I'm so sorry." Tayla stretched out her arms.

"Are you? Really?" Tiki paused midstep. "Because I've tried calling you five times in the last month. When you do actually answer my calls, after about two minutes you have to race off to deal with some work emergency and you promise to call me back. But you never do, even when I tell you that I need you."

"This is what you wanted to talk to me about?" Tayla asked.

"It doesn't matter if it was about what Josh did or if it was to talk about kittens and how cute they are. The point is you weren't there for me. You're never there for me or anyone. You only think about yourself." Tiki swiped at her cheeks.

"That's not true. If you had told me what was

going on, I would have listened," Tayla said. "Does Tonya know?"

"No. She doesn't, and I don't want to talk about this right now. Excuse me." Tiki bolted for the house.

"Shit. I better go after her," Tayla said. "It was nice meeting you."

"You too." Gael planted his hands on his hips and sucked in a deep breath. He turned and faced the lake. The white moon cast its eerie glow over the ripples the cool breeze created on the water. An engine off in the distance hummed. The moment he'd stepped onto this little piece of heaven, he'd felt a pull to his past and a connection to his future.

His home on the lake gave him a sense of closeness to his family that he hadn't had when they were alive. He knew that sounded crazy and maybe that was his guilt speaking, but he believed he was meant to be in this place.

At this time.

And Tayla needed him, if for no other reason than to help her understand that when doors close, people lock them, and they don't always let you back in. He was lucky that Greg had opened his heart in his grief.

He didn't have to.

Tayla was one weekend away from losing her sisters and Gael would do whatever he could to make sure that didn't happen.

∼

Tayla raced up the stairs to Tiki's childhood room, ignoring the shouts of her parents. "Open the door," she said as she tapped her knuckles against the wood. As kids, she and her sisters were close. Even when Tayla had gone off to college, she always made time for her younger sisters. Whatever they needed, she was there for them, so when Tiki had accused her of not being there?

Well, that stung like a million bees.

And Tayla didn't believe the words. She wasn't going to call Tiki a liar. That wouldn't be right. Or fair, under the circumstances. But the truth was Tiki chose not to inform anyone in their family what was going on.

That was on her.

The door squeezed opened, and Tonya appeared in the hallway.

"Did you know?" Tayla asked.

Tonya shook her head, stepping aside.

"I don't want to talk to you." Tiki sat in the

middle of the bed hugging a pillow.

"Don't take this out on her," Tonya said.

"Why not? She doesn't bother to even ask me what's going on. You at least called me or texted me regularly, trying to figure out what's been going on with me lately." Tiki swiped at her cheeks. "Tayla barely returns my messages."

"Yes, I do," Tayla said.

"I'm going to have to agree with Tiki on this one. You don't always. Sometimes we have to pester you."

Tayla sat at the edge of the bed. "I'm sorry. But I have a job that doesn't always allow me to take personal calls during business hours."

"But business hours for you are twenty-four seven," Tiki said. "It wasn't like I was asking you to drive up here or anything. I just wanted my big sister."

Tayla inhaled sharply, filling her lungs with as much oxygen as they would hold. She held her breath for a moment before letting it out with a swoosh. She and her family have had this argument before, and it never ended well. Honestly, she was tired of having it, which was one of the reasons she'd decided to take the vacation and come to the reunion.

She hoped that by doing so, she could go back to

work for a while and her family would leave her alone.

"Well, I'm here now and I'm sorry for what you've been going through." Tayla reached out and squeezed her sister's foot.

Tonya plopped herself down next to Tiki. "When did you find out he cheated?"

"About a month ago," Tiki said. "It started at the end of last summer and lasted two months."

"Jesus. What an asshole," Tayla mumbled.

"He justified the entire thing because for part of it we'd been having problems and we did break up for about a week." Tiki sighed.

Tayla hadn't known that, but she wasn't about to admit to it because both her sisters would jump down her throat for not being involved enough. And they wouldn't be wrong. Something that Tayla knew she needed to correct but wasn't exactly sure how to go about. Her career goals were so much more demanding. She wasn't putting down either of her sisters. Not at all. They both had followed their dreams. Done what they had set out to do and there was nothing wrong with their chosen professions.

However, what they chose didn't require the kind of time and dedication that Tayla's did. It was that simple.

"How did you find out?" Tonya asked, snuggling in next to Tiki.

"He actually told me," Tiki said. "I think he was afraid I'd find out and decided it was best if he came clean. He begged me to forgive him, and I tried. I really did. To his credit, whatever I asked him to do, he did, except for therapy. But every time I look at him. Hold him. Kiss him. All I see is her."

"I can't say that I blame you," Tayla said.

"No offense, but what do you know about relationships." Tiki glared. "When was the last time you even had a boyfriend?"

"I don't need to have one to have empathy for what my little sister is going through." Tayla kept her voice even and free of any lingering frustrations. This wasn't about her or even the fact her family was angry with her and her lack of communication. All that did was make her the easy target for Tiki and anyone else with a problem to take it out on.

"Have you ever been in love?" Tiki asked.

Tayla knew having a crush on Scott Saber when she'd been in the fourth grade didn't count.

Or even Bradly Quick for three years in high school.

Didn't matter she still thought fondly of both of them.

She dated in college, but no one stuck out. Not even now.

"Have you ever had someone rip your heart out, tear it into tiny pieces, then hand it back to you as if they hadn't done the one thing that they knew would hurt you the most?" Tiki asked with big, wet eyes.

"No," Tayla said. "I don't know exactly what that's like and I'm not pretending to."

"Neither am I." Tonya snuggled in next to Tiki. "I can't imagine what it would be like to have someone I love cheat on me. But I also can't imagine what it would be like to lose a child. None of us can and yet we can all agree we've done our best to be there for Foster."

"Don't go throwing my own words back at me." Tiki sighed. Loudly. "The thing is I've been so embarrassed about what happened."

"Oh, sweetie. There is no reason for you to be. He did this. Not you," Tonya said.

"I know." Tiki dropped her head back and folded her arms, hugging herself. "But Mom and Dad and his parents would drop hints about us getting married and everyone looked at us as if we were the perfect couple with the perfect little life. Well, it wasn't so f'ing perfect."

Tayla laughed. Tiki wasn't one to swear. Not even abbreviation swearing. It wasn't that she was little Miss Goody Two-shoes or anything. She'd done her fair share of being naughty, but in a clean way. If that made any sense.

Tiki was the kind of kid who bent rules, but never broke them. She wasn't a teacher's pet, but all authority figures adored her. If she did manage to find herself in the line of fire, someone handed her a bucket of water instead of calling the fire department.

"I thought maybe I could work through my feelings of betrayal," Tiki continued. "But all we do is fight and it's been getting worse and worse. Yesterday he gave me an ultimatum."

"No offense, but he has no business doing that," Tayla said with disdain dripping from every syllable.

"We can agree on that point." Tiki rested her head on Tonya's shoulder.

"I have to know. What was the ultimatum?" Tonya asked.

"We get engaged or he walks." Tiki held up her hand. "I told him that wasn't going to happen. I wasn't ready for that, and he then told me I had two weeks to figure it out. That's what we were arguing about tonight. His timeline on my getting over his infidelity and moving on with our plans to get married by the end of summer. I told him I needed more time and that we needed counseling and that's the one thing he is refusing to do. And that's my deal breaker."

"Good for you sticking to your guns." Though therapy wasn't something Tayla could see herself doing either. The idea of chatting about her most inner personal thoughts with a complete stranger made her prickle worse than having to share her emotions with friends. "Boundaries are so important." Tayla sprawled herself out on the bottom of the bed and stared at the ceiling fan. It didn't move, but it reminded her of when they were little girls, and they'd have sleepovers in each other's rooms.

They'd grab their blankets and spread out on the bed or the floor and talk for hours.

Tayla had to admit, she missed those days.

"Did you really just say that?" Tonya gave her hip a little kick with her foot. "Do you hear how cold and insensitive that sounded in this particular situation?"

"No." Tayla turned, narrowing her stare. "What is wrong with the discussion of letting people know what's appropriate and what's not when it comes to your personal space?"

Tiki and Tonya both burst out laughing. They rolled back and forth, hugging themselves and gasping for air while Tayla pushed herself upright and contemplated what the hell was so hysterical. In the last two years it was like she barely knew her sisters anymore.

"Can I ask you something?" Tiki crisscrossed her legs and leaned forward.

"Of course," Tayla said.

"Do you have *appropriate boundaries* at work? Because it seems to me like you don't know how to set those," Tiki said.

Tayla blinked. "How did we go from not allowing a cheating asshole like Josh to dictate whether or not he's out of the doghouse to my career? They aren't even remotely the same thing."

"But they are," Tonya said. "Kind of."

"Explain to me how." Tayla had to hear this one.

"It's simple," Tiki started. "You're right. It is good that I held my ground and didn't cave no matter how much I still love Josh. And it's going to take me a long time to get through this. I don't know if we would make it with therapy, but the fact he's not willing to sit on a couch for an hour once a week for a few months tells me he's not exactly the man I thought he was. That is a boundary. Something that you don't do."

Tayla wanted to tell her sisters she'd been trying to do that with her family for the last couple of years, but she figured that would just piss them off and that was the last thing she wanted to do. However, she did need to stand up for herself. "That's a false statement."

"Oh. No, it's not. When it comes to work, you let your boss walk all over you. If she says jump, you don't just jump. You perform a stunt so spectacular the world has to notice," Tonya said. "For you, a boundary is handed down from Anna Declay. It's whatever she wants and needs. Nothing else matters."

"That's not true." Tayla's heart thumped in the center of her throat like a frog calling its mate. It was thick and loud, and it got stuck there like a piece of food that had gone down the wrong tube.

"All we're saying is that you are allowing this job —and your boss—to treat you poorly," Tiki said. "How many times has Anna screwed someone over? How many times has she done it to you?"

Tayla tugged a few strands of hair from behind her shoulders and twisted them through her fingers. Her business could be cutthroat. If you wanted to get ahead, you had to be willing to play ball. It wasn't always pretty. Not everyone got to get on base. And only a select few hit it out of the park.

Tayla had started out wanting to be the one. She took the job with Anna Declay Designs knowing that most of the rumors about Anna were true. Matthew had warned her that Anna could crush her dreams with a snap of her fingers. That if Tayla even looked at her cross-eyed one day, that could be it. Dream over. She'd been embarrassed by Anna in front of the other designers when she'd first started working. There had been times she'd felt so shitty about her work and her job she thought about quitting.

She'd told Matthew no one deserved to be treated that way.

Then one day, out of the blue, Tayla's design was praised, and her world was changed forever. She was the it girl. Anna's pride and joy. One mistake—or perceived mistake—and Tayla's career would be garbage.

And not just at Anna Declay Designs.

Anna would make sure Tayla didn't work anywhere in the fashion world.

Something her sisters didn't understand.

"This is different," Tayla said. "This is my career.

It's everything I've ever wanted."

Tiki tilted her head. "But at what cost? Because not only are you putting space between us, but you're also not the same person."

Tayla knew her sisters were right and yet she couldn't admit it completely. Not to them. Not out loud. "This part is temporary. Once I get—"

"You've been saying that ever since you took this job," Tonya said. "It's always something. There's always a next thing. You're getting lost and so is your vision. You need to slow down. Promise us right now you're not going to leave Monday. That you will at least take one week." Tonya held up her index finger. "One week. Not two. One. If you really can't take the full two weeks, fine, but give us this week. Okay?"

"Do you know what pisses me off right now?" Tayla asked but didn't give either of her sisters a chance to respond. "Neither of you are taking time off. Just me. Why is that?"

"I'm getting into the height of wedding season," Tonya said. "You know that, and you also know that I've cleared my schedule as best I could."

"And for the record, I didn't take time off because I only get so many vacation days and I was supposed to take a trip with Josh, but I don't know if that's going to happen," Tiki said. "Not to mention I didn't think you'd show your face." She shrugged. "Just saying."

"That hurts." It might sting, but Tayla knew her sister spoke the truth. "Okay. I can commit to a week." However, try as she might, she couldn't ignore the whisper in her ear that told her it was exactly the same and Anna Declay was going to screw her over. "But you have to meet me halfway. I need to be able to work on my designs."

"Not during family time," Tiki said. "That means you can work when we work. But if we are here, or we make plans, you show up."

"That's reasonable, but I get to look at my phone occasionally," Tayla said.

"With permission." Tonya held out her fist. "Do we all agree?"

"I do." Tiki added her fist.

"I'm in." Tayla hit her sisters' hands. "And before either of you say anything, I swear I won't go back on my word." A light flickered outside.

Gael.

She sighed. If her sisters weren't spending the night, she'd be sneaking out to see if Gael might be interested...

No. She couldn't break her golden rule.

Could she?

4

Gael started his day telling himself he was going to research start-ups. But he ended up spending the entire afternoon staring at articles about Anna Declay and he didn't like anything he'd read.

Sure, she was a talented designer and her clothing line received rave reviews, but no one in the industry seemed to like her or her business practices. Ex-employees either signed nondisclosure agreements, which made Gael think something negative happened.

Or they went on every blog, podcast, or television show that would let them air their dirty laundry.

And boy, was it dirty.

Even the people who had nice things to say about Anna's work didn't particularly like her as a human.

The other part of his afternoon he spent Googling Tayla.

A task he wasn't proud of.

There wasn't too much information out there on Tayla. A few social media accounts. Information about where she worked. Stuff like that.

Nothing negative.

And nothing that tied her to Anna outside of the fact she worked for Anna Declay Designs.

He stepped outside and the cool spring air filled his nostrils. Slowing down his life, he'd learned to appreciate the little things. One of them was sitting in front of a fire. Something Piper loved, especially on a night like tonight.

It wasn't too cold, but the temperatures required a sweater. A few big puffy clouds floated across the dark sky lined with bright stars. The white moon cast a glow on the still water below. It was a night like these where the emptiness crawled into his heart and took up residence. There was nothing he could do to shake it. The best thing for him was to embrace it.

Greg told him it was important to feel the

emotions. Not to let them fester in the center of his gut. Or marinate in his mind. That would be unhealthy. But if he could manage to let the feelings flow through his system while remembering the good parts of Piper and his parents and the better memories of their relationships, he'd find peace.

Eventually.

Gael had to admit, all of Greg's methods were proving to be helpful.

Next door, people had started to arrive for the big reunion. Tessa and Tobias had apologized a dozen times for all the cars that would be on the property as well as the tents.

He told them he didn't care. That he welcomed it and at the time he did. He wanted to see their family enjoy their reunion. He thought it might be therapeutic. That it might help him heal his soul to see families living in the moment. Bonding, laughing, and sharing a private joke.

But right now, it hurt his heart. His nephews would never have this with their mom. Maybe Greg would remarry. Perhaps they'd have an amazing stepmother who would have this awesome family and something like this would be possible. However, it would never happen with Piper. With his parents.

Those days were gone.

He rubbed his eyes as he glanced over his shoulder. Four tents had been pitched in the yard between the houses. A couple of kids ran around, giggling and trying to catch fireflies. He'd missed out on so much and he had only himself to blame. He could never get that time back, but he could make changes so that he'd never be the man who had more important things to do on his nephews' birthdays. Or on holidays.

Or any other important occasion.

He strolled down the path and headed toward the water, contemplating a late-night boat ride. He leaned against the tree at the top of the dock. A couple waves crashed into the breakwall. The smell of fresh water mixed with the summer night air filled his lungs. He held his breath, holding the scent for as long as he could.

It reminded him of his childhood and all the evenings he and Piper had at summer camp. He cherished those memories like they were worth a million dollars.

"Hey," a familiar sweet voice rang out.

He turned and smiled.

Tayla stood a few feet away with her long hair cascading over her shoulders. She wore a pair of jeans and a long sweatshirt that went down almost to her knees. "What are you doing out this late?"

"It's only nine at night," he said. "Shouldn't you be with your family?"

She stuffed her hands in her pockets. "Tiki and Tonya took different cars to pick up relatives at bus stations and airports. I've been told to come over and remind you that you're invited to join us tomorrow." She held up her hand. "And that other people in the neighborhood are coming, so you won't be the only nonfamily member."

"Come with me." He stretched out his arm.

"Where am I going?" she asked.

"To have a drink with me." He took her hand and tugged. "I have a cooler on the boat."

"Okay," she said. "But only one."

"Fair enough." When he bought the place, he had LED lights placed on the path from the house to the waterfront. He worried that when the boys came, and it was dark, they'd end up falling in the lake because they wouldn't see it. It certainly came in handy for adults. "How is your sister, Tiki, doing?"

"Surprisingly well, but I think she's putting on a brave face for the family."

"Has she said anything more about Josh and what happened?" It wasn't really his business, but

Greg told him when engaging in conversation with people, Gael should try to focus on personal things, not work things. Even though Maxwell had asked him to help Tayla with her goals worksheet, tonight wasn't the time or place to bring it up.

"Josh called her first thing this morning. He doesn't want to break up and asked if he could come. Tiki told him no. He then asked if she would tell everyone that he had some work thing or make another excuse for him."

"Is she going to do that?"

Tayla let out a long breath. "Yeah, but she says she's doing it so she doesn't have to deal with all the questions and pity looks."

He took Tayla's hand and helped her onto his cruiser. "I don't blame her there. That would be a lot."

"I guess so." She glided her fingers across the back cushions. "This is a mighty fine boat."

"Thanks. I've only had her out twice." He opened the cooler and pulled out two vodka seltzers. "This is all I have out here. I hope it's okay."

"Perfect. I love these." She took a seat and cracked it open, chugging half of it. "That hits the spot."

"Long day?" He laughed.

"You have no idea." She stretched out her legs.

"Do tell." He lifted her feet and sat down, resting her legs in his lap.

She didn't refuse.

"My family did give me some space to work, but they hover. My mom wants to see my designs and I don't like doing that until they are done. Besides, they won't be mine. They will be owned by the company I work for. I have to be careful with all that and they don't understand."

"They want to be a part of your world." He set his drink on the small table and rested his hands on her ankles. He squeezed gently, moving over her shins and down over the top of her feet. "I've only been their neighbor for a few months, but they talk about you all the time."

"I'm sure it's not always in a good light."

"No. It is. However, they do miss you. They do wish you came around more often."

"It's hard to get up here sometimes, but when I do, I sure enjoy the peace and quiet." She wiggled her toes. "Do you always give foot massages to random women?"

"You're not random."

"I suppose."

"Would you like me to stop?" he asked.

Her blue eyes sparkled like diamonds under the light from the moon. "Absolutely not," she whispered. "I have a confession to make."

"I'm listening."

She set her drink next to his and leaned forward, palming his cheek. "I don't want to talk."

"I see." He breathed slowly, contemplating if he was going to push her away.

Or pull her close.

He wanted her. He had from the moment he'd laid eyes on her. No doubt about that.

She scooted closer, straddling his legs.

"I guess I don't have to ask what you want." He gripped her hips, holding her steady, staring into her warm blue orbs. He could get lost in them all night long. "Only, I'm not sure this is a good idea."

"It's not a bad idea." She kissed him. Hard. With intent. Their mouths melded together like the sun rising in the morning sky. As if they were old lovers greeting each other for the first time in a long while. It was hot and passionate and he wanted more.

He groaned. There was no way he'd have any self-control around Tayla.

"I can't give you more than a night. Or two. A fling." He cupped her face, fanning his thumbs over her high cheekbones. It was important that he be honest. Not only with her, but with himself. He wasn't capable of deep, meaningful relationships. Not yet. Not until he figured out the next part of his life. "I don't want more than that." She smiled, running her fingers through his hair. "My career and mending things with my sisters are my focus." She paused to kiss him gently.

She tasted like honey and smelled like sunshine.

"But does that mean I can't have a little something for myself?" She dropped her head to his shoulder. "God. I just heard that and you must think I'm the most selfish human being in the world." She shifted as if to get off his lap.

"Oh no, you don't." He held her steady. "You're not being selfish." He tilted her chin up. "At least not in the way you think you are."

"What does that mean?"

He traced a path down the angle of her jaw. "You're going through some emotional stuff with your family and you're under pressure at work. Of all the people here, I can relate."

"I'm sorry. I shouldn't—"

He pressed his finger over her lips. There were a million and one reasons why they shouldn't be together. "Don't be sorry." He pulled her tight to his chest. His hands dug into her back muscles, forcing her to arch into him as he brought his mouth to hers in a kiss that would seal the deal.

No more talking.

No more deciding whether this was a good idea or not.

It didn't matter.

They were adults. The only consequence they would face would be a potential slight awkwardness in the morning. However, he was sure they could handle it.

He stood.

"Whoa. What are you doing?"

"Taking this into the cuddy where it's a little more private."

"Oh. Good idea." She released her legs that had been wrapped around his body and turned.

He followed her down into the cabin. His boat was equipped with a small kitchen and one bedroom. It wasn't huge, but it wasn't tiny either.

She turned, lifting her large sweatshirt over her head. Her hair tumbled over her bra as she tossed the article of clothing at him, laughing.

As quickly as he could, he kicked off his shoes, ripped off his shirt, and stumbled out of his jeans, mesmerized by the woman standing in only a tiny thong.

He swallowed as he wrapped his arms around her waist. "You're beautiful."

"Why, thank you." She ran her hands over his shoulders, down the center of his chest, pushing him back. Her gaze lowered and she bit her lip. "I'm liking what I see." She kissed his stomach.

Never before in his life had he growled.

But he did.

His vision blurred. He threaded his fingers through her hair. He thought about stopping her, but he didn't have the strength as she lifted her gaze, catching his.

Her fingers curled around him, gently at first, increasing pressure while her lips danced over him in a wild tango.

His breath stuck in his throat. He couldn't suck it in, nor could he exhale. All he could manage was a series of gasps. Gripping the table by the door to the bedroom, he rocked with the few waves that gently moved the boat.

Nothing in his life could compare to this experience. Nothing.

Every single muscle in his body quivered.

"You have to stop."

"I was just getting started." She wiped her lips as she slowly stood with a wicked smile.

He was going to enjoy making her call his name. Opening the door, he pushed her back onto the bed, which took up most of the room. Looping his fingers into the elastic of her panties, he tugged them down her legs. He stared at her, running his finger from the inside of her ankle, up her calf, across her knee, and to the inside of her thigh.

She wiggled breathlessly. "Yes," she managed. "Please. I want you."

He leaned over and took one of her nipples in his mouth, sucking hard.

"Oh, God. Yes." She cupped his head, wrapping her legs around him, lifting her hips.

He reached between them, slipping a finger inside, teasing her with each gentle stroke. There was a sense of desperation to please her in ways he'd never experienced before.

Sex had been an act.

Something he did because it's what grown-ups who were attracted to one another did when they got horny.

This went way beyond that. It was more than a physical need. More than desire or passion.

It was the accumulation of all those things and something he couldn't quite put his pulse on.

"Please," she begged. "I need you."

He wasn't going to make her wait a second longer. He thrust himself inside her and if he could become drunk on a person, he was completely intoxicated now. He'd lost all control.

"Gael," she whispered. Her body jerked. "Oh. My. God." Her orgasm tore from her body and his followed in seconds.

They stared into each other's eyes for a long time. Their breathing ragged. Shocked at the intensity of their lovemaking. Of the moment they'd just shared. His heart beat so fast he wasn't sure it would ever calm, but it finally did.

He rolled to his side and pulled the blanket over their bodies. He held her close, running his hand up and down her biceps. He still hadn't really caught his breath as his lungs burned each time he filled them with air.

"Wow," she managed.

"That single word is certainly good for my ego."

She propped herself up, resting her arms on his stomach, then she kissed his chest. "Shall I repeat it?"

"I wouldn't stop you."

"I certainly don't regret coming over."

He chuckled. "I'm pretty happy you showed up

too." He kissed her shoulder. "But is your family going to start missing you soon?"

She sighed. "They might send out a search party and I don't think we want them to find us like this."

"Nope. We don't." He rolled to his side. "But do you have to race out right now?" How pathetic and needy did he sound? Geez.

"I can stay a few minutes. But we should put some clothes on, just in case."

"Let me find them for you." He scooted from the bed and found them. While he got dressed, he tried not to think about what tomorrow might bring.

Or even the next few minutes.

He wouldn't regret what had just happened, but he suspected she might. Or at the very least, she wasn't going to allow it to happen again.

He'd have to be okay with that.

He should be encouraging that.

"Why don't we go back up to the aft deck?" he suggested.

"Sounds like a plan." She adjusted her sweatshirt and scurried up the stairs. "It's such a pretty night."

"I couldn't agree more." He found his beverage and chugged. Leaning against the side of the boat, he took her into his arms. "How about one more kiss before you turn into a pumpkin?"

She laughed. "My sister's car just pulled in." She brushed her lips quickly over his mouth. "I better go. I promised Tiki I'd be there for her, and she's been all over the map since she and Josh broke up."

"I understand. Family first."

"Thanks for that," she said. "I'll see you tomorrow?"

"You can count on it." He helped her to the dock. "Walk home safely."

"Good night, Gael."

"Good night, Tayla." He stood in his front yard and watched her scurry across the grass.

He was in over his over his head and he wasn't sure what to do about it. He liked her. No question.

But even if he were ready to be in a relationship, she wasn't the right person because she would break his heart.

~

TAYLA ZIPPED up her sleeping bag. She couldn't believe she agreed to sleep outside in a tent. The last time had been when she'd been in college and even then it had been a stretch for her to do it.

"It's freezing out here," Tonya said as she pounded her pillow. "Whose idea was this?"

"Yours." Tiki glared. "We could have had a slumber party in one of our bedrooms, but nooooo, you decided to give up all our rooms for Mom's distant relations whom we don't know, much less like."

"Shhhhh," Tayla said. "Someone will hear us. These tents are made of fabric."

"We're practically in Gael's yard. Everyone else is over there." Tonya pointed. "We're fine."

"Speaking of Gael. What were you doing over there when I got home?" Tiki asked with a snarky tone.

"Reminding him he's invited to tomorrow's festivities. Like Mom asked me to." There was no way Tayla could tell her sisters what happened, even though she really kind of wanted to and in the past, she would have absolutely confided in her sisters. She had always trusted them with her secrets. Not once had either of her sisters ever betrayed her confidence. Sure, they'd hurt her feelings, and she was sure she'd hurt theirs, but when it came right down to it, her sisters were her lifeline. They were the only two people on the planet whom she knew without a doubt she could count on.

And part of her felt bad she wasn't trusting them with what had happened between her and Gael.

"You have a crush on him, don't you?" Tiki teased.

"Of course she does," Tonya said.

"He is hot." Tayla decided to play into the banter. It would make her life easier. And she could talk about him, how she was attracted to him, without having to spill the beans.

God. She missed talking to her sisters. Telling them her deepest, darkest fears. Her innermost personal thoughts. When it came to work, she had Matthew. She could confide in him almost anything.

But he wasn't Tonya or Tiki.

"And he's kind. He's a good listener. I've enjoyed spending time with him," Tayla added.

Tiki jumped to a sitting position. She gathered her sleeping bag around her waist. "You're not telling us something."

Heat rose to her cheeks.

"You've been home for two days and you've already seduced the neighbor." Tonya shook her head. She tugged off another piece of a twirler and put it in her mouth. "Unbelievable."

So much for keeping it a secret. Maybe she could continue to deny. "I did no such thing."

"The flushed look on your face says something completely different," Tiki said.

Tonya rose up on her elbows. "Was it more than cuddle kisses? Was there heavy petting involved? Do we anticipate this happening again?"

It was like they were all little girls again and they were gossiping about what happened on the playground.

She loved it.

Being catapulted back into her child for one night was exactly the distraction she needed. Tomorrow morning, for a few hours, she'd have to sneak away and work. She knew it wouldn't go over well, but she had to do it.

Balance.

Sleeping outside meant she'd wake up early. She'd already pulled her stuff out of her bedroom and put it in the alcove upstairs. She'd claimed that area and she'd been promised she'd be left alone.

"You're bombarding me with too many questions at once." Tayla fluffed her pillow and rolled to her back. Their tent had a screen skylight and it allowed her to view the stars in the sky, which only served to remind her of Gael and their evening. "I don't even remember what you asked me now."

Tonya kicked her thigh.

Tayla giggled like she used to when she was in high school.

"Is he going to be your boyfriend?" Tiki asked. "Because that's the only real important piece of information that we need to know."

Tayla blinked. She hadn't had a boyfriend in a couple of years. At least not a traditional one. She dated. Or she had friends with benefits. But since she started working for Anna, she stuck with the latter and it had been less frequent that she called on those friends.

"No," she said, slamming herself back into the reality of her life. "We flirted. We kissed. It was fun. But right now, my life is my career and he's got his own issues."

"Damn, you're a buzzkill." Tiki sighed and flopped back down onto her mattress pad. "Shit. That's hard. Next time we have a family reunion, we keep one of our rooms."

Tayla rolled over, hugging her pillow.

"You like him." Tonya squeezed her shoulder.

"Of course I do," she admitted. "But he lives here and I live in the city. That's a four-hour difference. And there are a dozen other reasons I can rattle off on why he and I aren't a good idea."

"Sometimes good things come out of bad decisions," Tiki said. "Isn't that what Grandma used to always say?"

Tayla laughed. "It sure is, but this is not one of those times." She tucked her hands under her cheek and closed her eyes. Soon she'd be able to make her life her own, and then maybe she'd be able to make room for romance.

5

Tayla made her way down to the waterfront after spending the majority of the morning and the first part of the afternoon in the alcove.

Working.

And daydreaming about Gael.

He seeped into her mind like a snake slithering through tall grass. She tried every trick in the book to remove every thought of Gael, but every single time she believed she'd been successful, a song came on the playlist that reminded her of him. Or a color she worked made her think of his eyes. Or the shirt he'd been wearing the last time she saw him. It was eternally hopeless.

Regrets crept into her mind. She worried that he

would look at her differently. Or that things would be awkward around her family when he was around and that was the last thing she wanted.

But she couldn't allow anything to happen between them again.

That rule had been in place for a reason. Breaking it had been a mistake. It was affecting her focus and that she couldn't have.

She sat down next to her grandfather and dipped her toe into the frigid waters of Lake George. It would be weeks before the temperature was warm enough to go swimming. At least for her, but it didn't stop others from waterskiing, tubing, or enjoying other water activities as her father drove past with a few of her distant relatives hanging off the tube behind the boat, waving and laughing.

She had to admit, she missed summers in Upstate.

She and her sisters used to sit on the dock and chat about anything and everything for hours. The conversations always started with boys. Who they liked or who had eyes for them. They gossiped about their friends. They shared their fears and concerns about the future.

When Tayla left for college, they'd promised

each other that as adults, they'd always come home as often as possible.

Tayla had been the only one to move out of the area.

And currently, she wasn't living up to her end of the bargain.

Last night had reminded her of what she'd been missing with her sisters. Not so much the sleeping in tents. That she could do without. But the family time. The connection.

She missed that and she would do better.

If only she could nail down this line. If Guy Contra bought her line, that was it. She'd be able to break out of the back in a few months. That's all she needed.

She hoped.

"How ya doing, Grandpa?" She leaned her shoulder against her grandfather's arm. When she'd been a little girl, her granddad had been her hero. She idolized him and she still did. He'd been the one she went to when she wanted advice on how to tackle most things in life. Even boys. He always had the best insight. Even when his words fell short or what he suggested didn't work, it was well worth the attempt.

"I'm doing," he said with a kick of his feet,

splashing the cool water into the air and laughing. "As much as it reminds me of your uncle, I'm glad to see everyone having a good time. This property was meant for family. I just wish we still had all three lots for you girls."

She could remind him that she lived in New York City and that she would most likely never move back, but why upset him further. Family was everything to her grandfather.

And to her parents.

To them it was the heart of the universe. Without family, nothing mattered. Family was the cornerstone and everything else was white noise.

"But then we wouldn't have Gael as a neighbor," her grandfather continued. "He's quite the gentleman. And handsome." Her grandfather waggled his brows. "I heard you were over there last night a little longer than necessary to extend an invite. Do I need to give you a lecture on being a lady?"

She rolled her eyes. "Are you gossiping now too, Grandpa?"

He laughed. "No. However, I am curious as to what's brewing there because he'd be quite the catch and I'm not blind. I see the way you look at him."

"Oh. So, you're being a matchmaker." She shook her head. She didn't want to lie to her grandpa. She loved him and normally he would be the go-to for dating questions. Her friends in high school and even college had all thought that was weird. But it would have been stranger to seek that intel from her parents. At least in her eyes.

"Are you telling me you're not interested?"

"It's not the right time for me. Or for him."

"And you know this how?" her grandfather asked.

"You're as bad as Mom."

"Your mom is a smart lady and she knows a good man when she sees one." He winked. "She married your father, didn't she?"

"Not the point. Did you know she invited Foster to this reunion? All that does is torture Tonya."

"She doesn't invite him for Tonya's sake," her grandpa said. "Your mom has a big heart. She means well and both Foster and Gael have suffered great losses. I, of all people, understand how that creates a void in a person's soul. It's important to be surrounded by love and happiness. I know I would have been lost without your parents and you girls after your uncle died. All your mom is doing is trying to help both Foster and Gael."

"I know, but sometimes she's a bit much. I mean, she's making things worse for Tonya. Foster's a great guy, but he's broken. He's never going to fall for Tonya."

"Never say never, child." Her grandfather batted her nose.

"Well, Tonya in this perpetual state of loving a man who won't love her back. It's not fair."

"We don't know if that's true or not. Besides, Foster keeps coming around. They do spend a lot of time together without anyone poking or prodding." Her grandpa smiled. "Did you get all your work done?" he asked, successfully redirecting the discussion.

She wasn't sure if that was a good thing. Or a bad thing.

Her grandfather often had an agenda when he did things like that.

"I'm getting closer," she said. "Thank you for asking."

"Your work has your parents in a tizzy." Her grandpa leaned back on his hands and glanced toward the sky. He'd always been a quiet, contemplative man. He talked slowly and chose his words carefully. Sometimes it was painful to have a conversation with him because of how long it would take him to carry on his side. She once asked him why he was so deliberate and his response had been he was waiting for the spirits to help guide him.

For as long as she could remember, her grandfather had believed his late son, Teddy, spoke to his heart. That he could feel his presence.

He said the same thing about her grandma, only lately it seemed all Grandpa did was wait around for the dead to communicate.

"You came down for breakfast, but didn't eat with them," her grandfather said.

"I thought it was best if I got all my stuff done so I could enjoy the party and be with family for the day."

Her granddad glanced at his watch. "It's two in the afternoon and you're just coming down now."

"Not exactly." The last thing she wanted to do was argue with anyone in her family. This party was going to last for two days. There would be tents set up all over two yards for kids and some adults to sleep in. Others would stay in an Airbnb down the street. And more at hotels down the road. Only a few would be leaving tonight. Most weren't heading home until Sunday night. "But look." She tugged at her cover-up. "No pockets. That means no phone so I can't check messages."

He tapped at her wrist. "I'm not stupid. That thing gets email."

She sighed. He had her there. "I promise you. I'm not going to disappear today except maybe to go for a walk or paddleboard or something like that. I've done all that I can when it comes to work."

"Forgive me if I don't believe you." He reached out and pinched her cheek like he did when she'd been a little girl, giving it a good wiggle. "Don't let life be all work and no play. Don't learn that lesson the hard way." He jerked his head toward Gael's house. "You should talk to Gael. His life used to be all about work until tragedy showed him what he was missing."

"Grandpa. I hear what you're saying. What everyone is telling me. And I've made a commitment to come around more. To come home more often. However, if I don't try, I won't ever know if I have what it takes. I'll always wonder if I gave up too soon. I have to follow this all the way through."

"Do you?" He arched a brow. "Have you re-examined your goals? Your motivations. Have you rewritten your plans and where you see yourself in a year? Three years? Five years? You have to do that on a regular basis because as we age, our world views and what's truly important shifts. But if we have tunnel vision, we can't see the new things that are presented to us and how they might affect our realities."

Sometimes the way her grandfather talked gave her a headache. He said the same thing five different ways, and then he'd repeat himself. But he meant well. He wanted his family to be happy and healthy and most important, he wanted them to live their lives to the fullest.

He didn't want anyone he loved to miss out on a single thing. It was one of the reasons he ended up keeping the land after his son died. After he stepped out of his grief, he was reminded there were other people still living whom he loved and he needed to be present for.

That didn't change the fact that the loss of his son created a moodiness about him. A dark cloud hovered over him, waiting to unleash a storm, only it never did. It was only a threat. It never happened. Her grandpa said he made a conscious choice every day to live life to the fullest. That's how his wife and son would have wanted it.

"My goals have not changed. I still want the same things."

"That may be true. But you need to look at them and how your career and life is aligning. What have you accomplished and how did you do it? Are you keeping track of that?"

"Well, no."

Her grandfather held her chin. "I know you're an adult and you think you've got this all figured out and maybe you do. But I want you to do me a favor."

"What's that?"

"I want you to write out a new plan. Like we used to do."

Oh shit. The last thing she wanted to do was spend hours upon hours going over goals, motivation, and tactical strategies for obtaining them with her grandpa. Of course she wanted to spend time with him, but not like that.

"And I want you to ask Gael to do it. He might be a financial advisor, but I hear he's brilliant when it comes to this stuff. I've sat down and talked to him a few times. He's seen the worksheets and he thought they were so well laid out that he wanted to use them for himself. So, it got me thinking and I talked to him about maybe helping you examine where your career is really going."

"Are you serious?"

"I am. Do this for me. Okay?" He gave her chin a little wiggle before dropping his hand.

"What if he doesn't want to do it with me?"

"You have wax in your ears, child. He's already agreed," her grandfather said. "So. Is that a yes?"

She knew her granddad and he wasn't going to stop until she agreed. "Fine. I'll do it."

"And share it with me."

Wonderful. She'd done this three times with her grandpa. Once in high school and it had been so much fun exploring her goals. Her dreams. All the things she aspired to be and how she planned on getting there. The best part had been presenting it to her parents who were impressed with her plan.

Her grandfather had her repeat this when she graduated from college and when she took her first job. Each time she saw the value in it and she appreciated what her grandpa had taught her. However, she was beyond the need to do it a fourth time. The stars had aligned.

"I'll get started on it and show you my progress later in the week. How's that?"

"I'll take it."

The dock rattled. She glanced over her shoulder and butterflies filled the pit of her stomach.

Gael strolled down the planks wearing only swim trunks. His dark, wavy hair curled at his neck. He smiled.

She swallowed.

Hard.

Damn, that man made her swoon like a teenaged girl at a boy band rock concert. Gael had that something special without even trying. He had swagger and he was the kind of man who didn't even have to try. She bet that he walked into a bar and both women and men stared with their tongues hanging out like a bunch of thirsty dogs.

"Hello, Gael," her grandfather said. "We were just talking about you and your skills in career planning."

"Oh, were you now." Gael laughed.

"How about you give an old man a hand to his feet," her grandfather said.

"Sure thing." Gael stretched out his arm. "It's a beautiful day."

"We couldn't have asked for a better weekend. But I need a little catnap and that hammock over there has my name on it."

"Sounds like a plan."

"You two enjoy yourselves," her grandfather said as he strolled down the dock with a slight limp.

His arthritis had been acting up lately and her parents had told her that he had more aches and pains the last few months.

Gael planted his hands on his hips. "Are you ready?"

"Ready for what?" She brought her attention back to the tall, sexy man who had been floating around in her mind all day, making it difficult for her to concentrate on anything.

"I was told you were waiting on me to go sailing."

The first thing that came to mind was that he hadn't acknowledged last night. Not even with a look. Of course, people were around, so she was grateful for that. But still. He could have at least winked or something.

The second thing that came to her mind was their Sunfish was currently occupied by one of her mom's cousins and their two little kids. They didn't have another sailboat.

"I'm sorry. You must be mistaken."

"No. I don't think so." Gael pointed toward his dock. "I was told you wanted to check out my catamaran."

She turned. Her face heated immediately as she stared at the cabin cuddy. His catamaran was moored about twenty feet from the dock.

"And who told you that?" Tired of craning her neck, she jumped to her feet.

"Your mom," he said slowly. He took her hand and ran his thumb over her skin.

She glanced down as heat raced across her muscles from his touch. "She actually told you that I said I wanted you to take me out on your boat."

"You came close to her exact words," he said.

"My mother is trying to set us up." She sighed. "And I believe my grandpa is in on it."

"I think that's been true from the moment you came home," he said.

"It's okay. We don't have to go."

"Do you like sailing?"

"I love it. But that's not the point. My family is trying to get us to go on a date."

He laughed. "I figured. But it's just a sail. Nothing more. Nothing less." He winked.

"If you don't mind, I would love to go out." She cleared her throat. "On your catamaran. I didn't mean on a date."

He offered his arm. "Now that we got that cleared up, let's go."

She slipped her hand into the crook of his elbow. "But now I have to ask. How do you feel about my mom and her little game, especially after what happened last night?"

He lowered his chin. "Which one of those things do you want me to respond to first?"

"How about being set up." Oh boy. That whole thing hadn't come out right.

"When I first accepted the offer of dinner the other night, I didn't think anything of it because I'd been invited more than once until I heard Foster had also been extended an invitation."

"You know him as well?"

He rested his hand over hers as they made their way off his dock and headed across her parents' front yard and toward his property. She did her best to keep her focus on the lovely boat.

Not the stares coming from the family members hanging out, playing Kan Jam.

"My sister and her husband got married up here and did the wedding boat drive with him. It was quite romantic."

"Foster's an old softy."

"I don't really know him, but I do know his boat service," Gael said.

"Tonya's a wedding planner and she hooks her clients up with Foster all the time. Swear to God, she talks people who didn't even ask for a wedding boat drive into it. But that's in part because she's in love with Foster."

"It kind of shows."

"Yeah. To everyone but Foster," Tayla said. "That said, I'm not sure Foster's of the relationship mindset anymore."

"Anymore?"

"Not my story to tell," she said.

"Fair enough." He helped her onto the boat before untying both the bow and stern. "Shall we go sailing?" He hoped on and started the engine, maneuvering the vessel out into the bay.

She settled onto the cushions and angled her face toward the sun. "You never answered my question about how you felt about what my mom did to get us out on this boat together."

"The first time you asked was in connection with what happened between us on my other boat." He increased the speed of the engine, setting out toward the open water. "Are you regretting it?"

"No. I'm sorry. That's not where I was going with this. It's just that I feel like everyone is pushing us together and—"

"The attraction between us is obvious," he said. "Are you worried about your family finding out?"

"You're going to think I'm a horrible person, but I don't want my parents to know. Last night, before anything happened, we both were okay with it being just sex."

He ran a hand over his mouth and down his chin. "I don't want to reduce what happened between us as something that didn't mean anything. I understand where you are in your career and chasing your dream and whatever last night was, or whether it ever happens again, it's not meant to be long term. We both know and accept that. Besides, I'm not in the best headspace after having lost my sister and parents."

"There is no timeframe on grief." She made sure no one from shore could see her as she palmed his face.

"It's honestly more than losing my folks and my sister. I'll have to live with that loss for the rest of my life. However, as your grandfather says, death is part of living. You can't avoid it. But there were other things going on in my life that I've had to face. Some hard truths that weren't pretty and I've needed to come to terms with them."

"That sounds kind of cryptic." She adjusted her ponytail as he cut the engine and went about raising the main sail.

"I don't want to bore you with the painful details," he said. "Now. There's not a ton of wind, but there's enough to put up the sail and cross our fingers."

She laughed. "I'm just happy to be outside in the sun."

"I hope you have sunscreen on because I don't have any on the boat." He tugged at the sheet and the white sail.

"I do." But she wondered if she should have lathered up a second time. She and the sun weren't always friends. She stretched out her legs and closed her eyes, letting all the sounds of summer fill her senses. Birds chirped in the sky above. Laughter echoed across the water.

This was the noise of her childhood.

"Yeah. This isn't going to work," Gael said.

She peeked open an eye as he rolled the fabric around the mast and tied it with the sheet. He pulled out a seltzer from the cooler. She took it and cracked it open. The watermelon flavor tickled her throat. "Oh. That's good, but this is not sailing."

"Nope. This is floating." He sat down across from her and smiled. "Sometimes, this is better."

"I wouldn't go that far, but just being out on the water is awesome."

"When I was a little boy, my sister and I used to

go to this camp over on the west side up across from Dome Island."

"Seriously? Me and my sisters used to beg our parents to send us to camp. But they would always say no. Their reasoning was that we might as well have lived at camp."

Gael tossed his head back and laughed. It was a rich noise and melted across her ears like butter melting over warm bread. "That's funny, but I can see how they would feel that way just watching all the activities today. I wish my nephews were here, but they are visiting Greg's parents for two weeks in Maine."

She raised her hand and waved to her dad as he drove by. Her family would have something to say about her being alone in a sailboat, that wasn't sailing, with Gael. It didn't matter that it had been her mom who orchestrated the entire thing. Tayla wasn't holed up in a room somewhere working.

She was with an eligible bachelor, behaving as though she could actually be having a good time.

"Can I ask you a question?" She had no right to pry, but her mind wandered back to the city. She either wanted to dress Gael in her designs.

Or undress him.

Sigh. That wasn't going to happen again.

"Sure."

"Do you miss city life?"

"Only when it's ten at night and I run out of something and everything that's open is like ten miles away," he said. "But other than that, no. Not really, which is weird because I used to think I'd die if I was ever forced to leave the Big Apple."

"I know that feeling, only when I do finally force myself to drive here, I remember all the reasons that make this place special."

"There is no other place on earth like it." Gael nodded. "Would you ever consider leaving New York City?"

"That all depends on where my career takes me once I get my own line." She thought about what her grandfather had asked her to do. When she'd graduated from college, one of her long-range goals had been to have her own line. And not with another designer. She wanted her own entire clothing line. A brand. Where she lived had not been a driving factor.

She knew she needed to start out in New York City. To get her education both in school and then in the fashion world. To learn the ins and outs of the business. To understand the way the fashion world worked and how she was going to fit into it.

However, as her mind mentally pulled up the business plans her grandfather wanted her to redo, she remembered one important detail about her goal that has shifted since she graduated from high school.

Her grandfather was a sneaky man and he knew it.

When she'd set out to have her own clothing line, it never had to be world famous. It didn't have to be on runways in all the major cities across the globe.

The goal had never been to be a household name.

It just had to be hers and she just had to get paid for it. She wanted to make a living at what she loved.

Simple.

When they redid the plans and adjusted her goals, she didn't adjust that. She'd been adamant that fame wasn't her gig. That making a living as a designer came in all shapes and sizes. She wanted to partner with someone who believed in her and that could be any number of businesses or people. Even musicians partnered with designers to build brands.

But she had to have a portfolio.

She had to have experience. That is what all this had been about, originally.

Experience and expertise.

And then she met Anna Declay and everything changed.

"What about where you want your life to take you?" He lifted his beverage to his lips and sipped. The condensation dripped off the can and onto his leg.

All she could think about was last night.

And licking that very spot.

Ugh.

"Right now, all I can think about is this one private showing. If I nail this and the client wants to buy the collection, he buys it most likely with my name on it."

"Wait a second. Most likely?" Gael set his drink on the fiberglass floor and leaned forward. "That doesn't sound like it's a done deal."

Shit. Poor choice of words. But true choice. And that sucked. "It's possible he hates my designs, and then nothing happens. Or he doesn't trust that my name alone will carry them and he demands Anna's name goes on them. And if Anna doesn't like them, she might not even show them to the client and she could take someone else's. There are a ton of other designers waiting to shove their work under Anna's nose. They could be doing it right now while I'm out of the office. It's that cutthroat."

"So, what you're saying is if she doesn't like them, you could be out and that means you've lost your shot to be… what? I thought you were already this woman's right arm."

Tayla sighed as she tilted her face toward the sun, soaking in the warmth of its rays. It was rare she discussed work with anyone. Except Matthew. But he understood. People outside the industry didn't get it. "I'm in her good graces. She likes me. She uses my designs more than she does anyone else's right now. That could all change. But this chance is different. This client is looking at me specifically. He and Anna have been discussing me and my designs. No time in the history of Anna Declay Designs has that happened."

"Okay. I understand that. But let's say it doesn't work out. There are other designers in the city. And in other cities. Can't you work for someone else while you work on your own collection?"

"It's not that simple." If it were, she would have done it already. "No one will take me seriously unless I have had someone like Anna give me a little credit for what I've done. Sure. I could go get a job and work on the line producing clothes and sketching for designers. But in order for me to even have a brand influencer be interested in wearing one of my designs, I need someone with clout to tell them to. Make sense?"

"Oh. Trust me. I get the game." Gael scooted to the other side of the boat, sitting so close she could feel the heat from his body rise off his skin and land on hers like a soft butterfly. "When I first started out in the financial advising business, I was telling my boss what stocks to buy for their clients. I was feeding them all the right tips and they were getting all the glory while I was treated like a nobody. I understand what it's like to have that carrot dangled right to the top of the ladder only to be stepped on by three other associates before being able to climb back up."

"If you get it, why all the questions?"

"I'm curious as to what your end game is," he said. "I wanted my boss' job. And when I got it, I wanted more. The problem for me became when I couldn't define what more looked like."

"You've been hanging around my grandfather too much and this is starting to sound like more of a different kind of setup." She pointed to the shore and her family home.

"I didn't mean to upset you," Gael said. "That

wasn't about you at all." He bent over and snagged his seltzer, downing it in one gulp. "Earlier when you said I was being cryptic, well, this is part of why I had to get out. I was addicted to the more part of my career. I couldn't get enough, but I no longer had vision. What I did have was desire—an overwhelming need to finish what I thought I had started, and it cost me my sister and her family before Piper died."

"I don't understand."

"The last year of Piper's life we barely spoke because she couldn't stand the person I'd become. I thought she was being petty and didn't understand the importance of what I was doing. I actually put down her doctor husband and her choice to help support that and be a wife and a mother." He glanced toward the sky. "I think my actual words were something like *taking care of kids is fine, but it's not like you're holding someone's livelihood in the palm of your hands. If I screw up, I could make or break someone for the rest of their life. What are you and Greg doing? Maybe if he was a surgeon or something, but he's not.*"

"Wow. No offense, but you suck."

"Trust me. I know what an asshole I was and if you ever need a psychiatrist, I hear my brother-in-law is an excellent one. Though he works in the hospital psych department. I guess that's some really hard-core stuff."

"I can only imagine."

"Anyway, Greg didn't like me much and up until about two months ago, he wouldn't let me be alone with his boys. He's been afraid I'll take a job as a financial advisor and run off to the city, breaking Benny and Sam's heart much like I did Piper's. Our last words to each other weren't kind."

"I'm sorry." She reached out and took his hand. "I hope you've forgiven yourself."

"I'm getting there." He squeezed. "The fact that Greg no longer constantly tells me that I should have died in that plane helps."

"Ouch. That's mean."

"It's true though," Gael said. "My parents begged me to fly with them to Florida, but I was too busy. I had a big fish on the hook. I had to close the deal. So I chartered a plane for my family. Piper was pissed. I never heard so many swear words come out of her mouth before. She told me if I didn't get on the plane with them, I would never see the boys again. I didn't believe her. I figured she was being overly dramatic and went about my business. I also ignored them the rest of the day and night. I heard about their deaths on the news while I was at a bar celebrating."

"Jesus." She turned, palming his cheek. His eyes were hidden behind his shades. But hers teared up something horrible. "I'm so sorry."

"I choose my actions and my words much more carefully now because of all that, but it haunts me and I figure it will for a long time."

"How are things with you and Greg now?"

"They're so much better, but he's still jaded and he worries. I can understand why. My track record stinks. But I'm making this my home."

"What about work?"

"That is a valid question and one I need to figure out, but whatever it is, this is now where my life belongs."

Tayla waved again as her dad drove past with her mom's aunt and uncle riding shotgun while two kids played king of the kneeboard. Her chest tightened for all that Gael had to endure. It was a lot to carry and something she took to heart.

She loved her sisters and she heard more clearly what they had been trying to tell her. Tayla could do better. She could be more present. She would re-examine her goals. Rewrite them as they fit into her life now. And then she'd make sure she allowed for family time.

It was a four-hour drive.

She could come to town on a Saturday afternoon and spend the night once every other month.

"It is a beautiful place to land," she whispered. "I need favor."

"We sleep together once and you're already asking for—"

She smacked the side of his shoulder.

"Ouch," he said.

She held up her index and middle fingers. "Now it's two favors."

"Okay."

"First. My sisters know we kissed," she said, covering his mouth with her hand. "I had to tell them something. I was gone a long time last night and while my parents bought the whole *I was chatting with him about life goals*, my sisters didn't. So be prepared for some harassing; just please don't give them any ammunition."

"All right. What's the second thing?"

"Okay. It's three things."

"That's going to cost you." He pressed his finger over her mouth when she opened it. "What? I can't tease when we're alone?"

"People are watching," she said.

He dropped his hand to his side. "Okay. What can I help you with?"

"My grandfather wants me to redo my goals and business plan. He's kind of big on those and I promised him I'd do it. If you wouldn't mind taking a look at them with me?"

"He told me about that and I'd be honored. What's the last thing?"

"I need to finish these designs I'm working on by Wednesday or Thursday and I was hoping I could maybe use a room in your house to finish them." She held up her hand. "I know it's a big ask, but I need a few hours each day of uninterrupted creative time to do it. But they will hover and pester and bother me endlessly and make it harder for me to spend time with them."

"I have an entire den at your disposal." He lifted his index finger. "But I have a condition."

"Dare I ask," she said.

"On calm mornings you kayak with me and on windy ones you sail. And maybe one day we do a hike up Buck Mountain."

"That kind of negates my first request."

"Oh, but you fail to understand that by spending time with me, doing those other activities, your family won't question why you're inside my house." He winked. "We'll have to manage our time and make sure it doesn't appear as if I'm hogging all of it, but if we do it right, you can have your cake and eat it too."

Her lips parted. Her hand involuntarily landed on the center of his chest. Her breath hitched as she tried to suck in more oxygen, but failed.

She had to admit, it was a brilliant plan.

"You don't mind?" she asked.

"As long as you hold up your end of the bargain, not at all."

She held out her hand. "It's a deal."

"Oh. We're not shaking on it." He leaned a little closer. "This deal needs to be sealed with something a little less cold." His lips touched hers, softly at first, but he quickly increased the pressure as he took her into his arms. His tongue eased into her mouth, twisting and swirling around hers like a wave rolling onto the beach, bringing with it all the things the ocean has to offer and stealing some of the sand.

The sound of a speedboat approaching reminded her that this might not go unnoticed.

"That wasn't too smart," she whispered, scooting backward.

"Kissing you is always a good idea." He wiped his mouth and adjusted his sunglasses.

"Oh. That's a line."

"I'll remember that." He turned on the engine and pushed the throttle into gear. "So, how about Monday morning we hike up Buck Mountain? Say, leave here at six in the morning and then afterward, you can use my den to get some work done."

"Thank you." She turned and touched her lips. The kiss still sizzled, sending hot pulses across her body.

"What are friends for?"

6

Gael stuck his head in the fridge and pulled out two beverages. He made his way through the house and stepped out onto the front patio. He glanced next door, mentally kicking himself for avoiding Tayla and everyone else in her family. He told himself it was because he didn't want to encroach on their family time. That if anyone should respect the importance of their reunion and what that meant, it was him.

Most of the guests had left and by this evening, it would just be Tayla, maybe her sisters, and her parents.

It had been a long time since Gael had wanted to spend time with a woman. Outside of taking her to bed and then sneaking out before the sun came up. He didn't do long conversations or romantic walks. Not since his first wife and even then he barely did it.

One of the reasons he was divorced.

Stacey had stuck it out with him for four years. None of which were good. At least not for her. Nothing about his life had changed after he tied the knot. He still did whatever he wanted and that hadn't settled right with Stacey.

Truth of the matter was he hadn't loved her the way a husband should love his wife. He cared about her a great deal.

But love?

Back then, he loved two things.

Money and power and Stacey couldn't give him either.

Tayla glanced up from behind her computer. She smiled and waved.

His pulse increased. Every time she graced his eyesight, his heart ached to spend more time with her. He didn't care if words were exchanged. All that mattered was breathing the same air.

It was a strange feeling for him and he didn't quite know how to deal with the conflicting concerns he had about her career life.

Because sitting with family while working wasn't being present emotionally. According to his mother, it was condescending and downright rude. Looking at it from this angle, he had to agree. He used to do the exact same things, pretending to engage in riveting conversation with his dad when in reality, he was only half there. His other half was thinking about what stocks he needed to tell his clients to buy and sell. Or what start-ups were good investments.

Nothing about what Tayla was doing right now could be considered quality time with family.

He raised his hand and wiggled his fingers before heading down toward the dock.

When he'd agreed to take Tayla sailing yesterday, he'd told himself he'd done so because Tessa had asked him to and because he genuinely wanted to help Tayla find balance between her career and her family.

Not because he wanted to steal a few more kisses and remind his body what it felt like to hold her in his arms.

He told himself that it was all about helping her so she didn't make the same mistakes he had. To show her that she had choices. That didn't mean her career couldn't be front and center. Work was still important, a concept he was learning from Greg.

"Here you go." He handed Greg a seltzer. "How are you holding up with the boys being with your parents without you?"

"I'm losing my fucking mind and it's only been two nights." Greg held up his can and clanked it against Gael's. "They will be back late tonight and I told them to keep them at their place and I'll pick them up after dinner tomorrow. But I haven't been away from the boys overnight since Piper died."

Gael's heart jumped to his nostrils every time he heard his sister's name and the words dead or death. It was still surreal. Even when he went to the gravesite, he half expected her to sneak up behind him or some such shit.

"I'm sure they miss you," Gael said.

"Oh, they do. But I think I miss them more."

Gael laughed. "When Piper and I went to summer camp, our folks complained that all the other kids wrote home more than we did. Our excuse was that we had each other so we didn't get homesick like the other children did."

"Piper told me you two wrote each other letters at camp."

"We did. It was the dumbest thing ever, but during rest hour after lunch, the counselors would tell us we had to write letters home, so we'd scribble notes to each other and then say our parents said we had to save on stamps and mail them together. Instead of doing that, we exchanged our notes so we'd have something to do the next day at rest hour."

"I've been waiting for the right time to tell you this, but she saved some of them and I found them the other day when I was cleaning out some stuff."

Gael choked on his beverage. He pounded his chest as he struggled for air. He had never been as sentimental as Piper and when their parents had sold the family home to downsize so they could travel when his dad had retired, Piper kept all their old keepsakes.

He told her to toss his out. He hadn't seen them in years; why would he want them now?

Well, he was glad she'd saved them.

"You okay?" Greg shifted closer.

"Fine," he managed. "Went down the wrong pipe." He inhaled slowly, trying not to cough. "She seriously kept those notes?"

Greg nodded. "I also found some pictures from when you were kids that I thought you might like. I made duplicates. I know you want the boys to have her childhood memories, as do I."

"I appreciate that. Thanks." Gael used to refuse

his sister's belongings. Not because he didn't want the memories, but because he wanted his nephews to have as much of their mother as possible. Now he planned on making more memories for them. A keepsake of some kind. He'd find a way to piece together her world in a new way. Create something the boys could look at and see all parts of their mom. He had no idea what yet. But he knew it would be spectacular. "Did you read the notes?"

"Sorry, man. I had to. I know that was stuff between you and Piper, but once I unfolded one, I couldn't help myself." Greg shook his head and laughed. "You two really were glued at the hips at one point."

"We were Irish twins. Ten months apart. About the only thing we didn't do together was play hockey. She came and watched all my games though."

"Only because she was in love with the goalie."

"Oh, my God. That's a moment I'd like to forget. I never understood that attraction, but she followed him around like a dog in heat," Gael said. "And he barely noticed. Piper begged me to talk to him, so one day I skated up to him after a game and asked him why he didn't like my sister and he informed me that he had a thing for me." Gael smacked his forehead. "I was only thirteen at the time. I didn't want to hurt my sister's feelings, but I didn't want to hurt his either. The fact that my sister accused me of stealing a potential boyfriend in front of some of our friends didn't help me in letting that goalie down easy."

"I heard he asked you to the winter dance."

"He did and in a very public way. He actually thought he had a chance. He assumed I just needed a little help coming out. I felt so bad telling that kid I had a girlfriend and he kept trying to tell me I didn't have to pretend anymore. It took almost two months for me to prove I was a straight teenager."

"That story still cracks me up," Greg said. "I used to not believe you could be so sensitive."

"I'm so glad I was able to amuse you."

"You know, we ran into that goalie a few months before Piper died. He's got a partner and they adopted a couple of kids. He lives in Glens Falls."

"That's cool."

"Too bad he wasn't single." Greg laughed.

"Oh. Aren't you funny." Gael turned his head. The two-day party next door had died down as the sun settled behind the mountains in the west. Most of the out-of-town family guests had packed up and headed back to whatever part of the world they came from. The few stragglers were saying their goodbyes.

He stretched his arms toward the sky. It was pushing seven on Sunday and he had an early date in the morning.

Well, he didn't dare call it that and he would have to learn to keep his hands and his lips to himself.

Tayla was dangerous.

Not just because she was gorgeous. And as sweet as honey.

But he found himself thinking about her constantly. He thought he could handle a fling. That's all he was capable of and that's all she could manage. He knew that without a doubt. She could barely handle taking time for herself. She wouldn't be able to balance a relationship.

And who was he kidding. He'd gone from working eighty hours a week to doing absolutely nothing. Talk about extremes.

"Can I ask you something incredibly personal?" Gael and Greg's relationship hadn't been good from the moment Greg started dating Piper.

Greg didn't like the way Gael put his family last

and Greg understood sacrifice. He had to make a lot of them to become a doctor. He missed holidays with his family. He worked long hours and double shifts. And before that, he studied his ass off in medical school. His life hadn't been easy.

But he always managed to find time for those who mattered.

"You can ask, but I might not answer. Or you might not like how I answer," Greg said.

"Have you thought about dating?"

Greg jerked his head. "No."

"I didn't necessarily mean right now. But someday. I mean, I know Piper wouldn't want you to sit on this dock getting old with me."

Greg burst out laughing. "You're right about that one. She'd be mortified by that thought. But as far as dating, I can't even think about that. And not just because I miss your sister. I have Benny and Sam to think about. I can't be introducing people in their lives who might not stick around."

Gael tapped his chest. That wasn't meant to be a jab, he knew that. But it still stung. "I know they need stability, but there's no reason for you—or them—to spend the rest of your lives alone."

"That's fair and maybe someday I will. But for

now, my focus is the boys. Work. And keeping this thing with us going. I know that Piper is smiling down on us. That us spending time together is the one thing she wanted more than covering up the few gray hairs she'd find." Greg smiled. "Now what about you?" He raised his seltzer in the direction of the Johnson place. "You keep looking next door and specifically at one woman. What's going on there?"

"Tayla." Gael had made a promise that he wouldn't lie to Greg. Not even about the silliest things. But especially about the things that made Gael uncomfortable, and chatting about emotions made Gael want to run and hide. Doing a deep dive about girls and love lives and all the touchy-feely things had become a struggle for him sometime after he'd gotten married.

Or maybe before.

He couldn't remember.

Those years had all been one big blur.

"The sister who lives New York City. She's here on vacation. We shared a moment. Or two."

"What does that mean, exactly?" Greg asked.

"There's a mutual affection for one another, only she's headed down the same path of destruction with her career that I went on if she's not careful."

"Are you sticking your nose where it doesn't belong?"

Gael watched Tayla climb in the canoe with Tiki. They pushed off the dock and paddled south, both giggling and laughing. Considering what had happened the other night, he was glad to see Tiki enjoying herself. "A little bit. However, she's asked me to help her with a business plan. Or more like a goal alignment worksheet. Something that she and her grandfather have done in the past. She gave me the ones she did in high school and college and they are impressive. She's impressive."

"So why do you think she's making the same mistakes you did?"

"Because I've lived next to her parents for a couple of months and I've listened to them complain about the same things my folks did about me. But it's more than that." Gael pushed his sunglasses on top of his head and kept his focus on the backside of Tayla while she used her paddle to maneuver the canoe through the water. "Especially now that I've seen what her goals had been when she set out on her career."

"We all shift as we get older," Greg said. "While I always knew I wanted to be a doctor, and in the mental health profession, I never expected I wanted to stay in emergency medicine."

"I get that." Gael nodded. "What struck me as interesting was the fact she penciled in family in all her plans. As in a husband and kids. But now she has no room for romance. Not until she gets her career where she wants it. Her goals in her previous plans boil down to making a living at being a designer and having control over her own designs. Having a brand. Not being a cog in someone else's machine."

"Are you saying she's moved completely away from that?"

"She doesn't believe so. She started out in her career wanting to learn every facet of the business so that when the time was right, she could break out on her own. She believes that this designer is going to give her that chance."

"That sounds reasonable," Greg said. "Everyone has to start somewhere."

"Only, I did a little research. She doesn't need Anna Declay Designs to create her own fashion line. As a matter of fact, that could hurt her in the long run because it could pigeonhole her into being a designer of just one kind of article. No. What she needs is vision. A plan. She needs to become her own brand. Create a signature style. Not bend over backward and immerse herself into someone else's. Of course, the final piece of that puzzle is the money to do the marketing and manufacturing."

"Oh no." Greg waggled his finger. "I can feel your adrenaline pumping. You want to invest in something that she doesn't even know if she wants to do."

"She wants to be her own brand. I know that for a fact." Gael folded his arms. But Greg was right about one thing. He didn't know how she wanted to go about doing it. Gael could spin his wheels all day long about what he thought Tayla should do, but that didn't matter. "Do you want to know what bothers me the most about what I found out online today?"

"Yes," Greg said.

"This Anna person is a lot like my old boss."

"How so?"

"She's had her own company for five years now. She's whispered three times she was going to pull someone from the ranks of her company and give them a shot, like her mentor did for her. Each time she did so was after a celebrity mentioned wearing a design that they'd chosen out of a private showing and Anna mentioned she was working closely with a young up-and-coming designer. But when it came time to give that designer a name, to bring them out into the spotlight, something happened. The first time the designer, according to Anna, left her company, stealing her designs and she was going to have to take legal action. She made such a big stink over it and went on every talk show. No one will work with that designer. The thing is, she didn't steal the designs. The second time she publicly shamed the designer for screwing up a show. That designer has since gone on a couple of shows to say that Anna lied, and Anna then filed a lawsuit and now there's a gag order. There are a few other instances inside the company where Anna has made a big deal about individual employees, only to pulverize them. I got that information from a blogger who used to work for Anna. She doesn't blog about it because Anna threatened her. Seems to be a thing. And now Anna is saying she's about to pull a designer out again, only this time she's been more publicly vocal about it."

"Let me guess. That designer is Tayla."

"It is and doesn't that remind you a bit of what my boss used to do to me when rich and famous clients would walk through the door?"

"It sure does," Greg said. "Dumb question, but does Tayla know about these other designers?"

"She does and she told me not to believe everything I read or hear. That she's been working with Anna now for two years. She knows exactly how Anna works and she's not concerned. But I don't believe Tayla. No more than any of you believed I'd ever make it home for Thanksgiving."

"This is not your problem," Greg said. "I can tell you're torn. I can also tell you have real feelings for her brewing deep under the surface. However, you barely know her and you still have a lot of work to do on yourself."

"I wish I could let it go. But between her—and Maxwell—asking for my help, not wanting her to ever have to live through what we have, and the fact that I kissed her and I fucking liked—"

"Okay." Greg shifted in his chair. "You really like this girl."

"She's under my skin, but I can't get involved with her no matter how much I want to."

"And why not?"

"You really have to ask that question?" Gael lowered his chin and raised both brows. "She lives in New York City, for starters. I can't ever go back there. Not even to visit. Not yet anyway. It's too soon and sometimes when someone randomly asks me for advice, I feel the pull so intensely I start to sweat."

"That's normal. You're wicked smart when it comes to finances. And there's nothing wrong with going back to that profession. On a much smaller scale. Kind of like what you're expecting Tayla to do."

"Nope." Gael shook his head. "That's entirely different. She hasn't fallen so far down the rabbit hole she can't climb out. All she needs is someone to show her what her original ideas were. That's why her grandpa asked her to revisit her goals. To rewrite them. For me, I took that entire thing too far. Besides, I don't want to go back. It would only serve as a reminder of what I lost and how I lost it. That's not a good place for me."

"Fair enough," Greg said. "I know you hate it when I put my doctor hat on, but why is pursuing her out of the question? Is it because she lives downstate? Is it her career? Or is it something else?"

"It's all of the above," Gael admitted. "But my biggest problem is my own fears."

"Of what?"

"Being on the receiving end of what I did to Stacey."

"Wow. That's insightful."

"I know how much I hurt her." Gael hadn't seen it during the marriage. Or even when she left. He'd been too busy with his career to give a fuck. But after Piper died and Stacey showed up at the funeral, they spoke and he noticed something about Stacey he'd never seen before.

How strong she was and he commented on his observation, which made her laugh. Not because she thought it was funny, but because she felt her strength came from having divorced his sorry ass. It was a pain that she had still been working through.

She'd seen him as the love of her life and he destroyed it slowly and methodically. She told him it would have been easier to deal with if he'd cheated on her.

Talk about a shocking statement.

"I don't ever want to do that to someone again, but I also don't want it done to me."

Greg reached out and squeezed his biceps. "When I met your sister, she was dating someone else. Do you remember?"

Gael nodded. "But you and Piper didn't hook up until after that ended."

"That's true, but that didn't stop me from pursuing her. I too can be a selfish prick. And I wanted Piper and I didn't believe for one second that idiot was going to make her happy."

"He was boring as sin." Gael remembered those

days well. Greg had come onto the scene just as Gael's career had started to take off. It had marked the shift in his perspective. His sister hated the city and Greg took a residency at Albany Medical and Piper followed. For about five minutes Gael missed his little sister.

But they still got together on weekends.

For a while.

"Listen," Greg started. "If you like her, why not at least find out more. Explore what you have in common while you're helping her figure out what her next steps are. It's not like you're investing weeks, months, or even years of your life into a relationship."

"I'm in unchartered waters," Gael admitted. "I feel like I'm losing my lifeline when it comes to her. It's as if I've already jumped off the cliff."

"You're aware of your emotions. That's a good thing," Greg said. "My advice would be to remind yourself of all your feelings going into each encounter and maybe keep a journal after and you can always call me."

"You might regret offering that."

Greg chuckled. "I already do." He stood. "I need to get going. I've got an early start tomorrow. Thanks for dinner."

"Anytime." Gael gave Greg a slap on the shoulder in a manly hug. Every day he thanked the universe that Greg had forgiven him for his shitty behavior. He never wanted to do anything to jeopardize that relationship again.

Life was too short.

7

"Don't do it." Tayla leaned against the hood of her sister's car and folded her arms. "I'm begging you. Tell him it's late. You have to work tomorrow. You don't have to be mean; just tell him no."

"I have no intention of taking him back," Tiki said. "However, I can't turn off my love for him and I want to hear what he has to say. I'm not doing it for him. I'm doing it for me."

Tayla realized she wasn't going to talk her sister out of it and because she was working on this whole balance thing and being supportive, perhaps she could skip out on spending more time with her nose in her sketchbook. "Would you like me to come with you?"

"No. If you showed up, he'd probably take off running. He's terrified of you. More so than anyone else."

"As he should be." Tayla laughed. "I have half a mind to cause that boy some bodily harm."

"Thank goodness your bark is worse than your bite." Tiki pulled open the car door. "Thanks for being here for me. It means the world to me."

Tayla hugged her sister. "You can call or text me later. If I'm awake, I promise to take the call. Hell, if you want me to, I'll make sure I stay up until I hear from you."

"Thanks. I appreciate that and I will message you when I get there and when I leave." Tiki smiled. "I want to see if you can keep the promise."

"Oh. A challenge. I love it." Tayla did her best not to be insulted by the jab. She didn't like that her sisters didn't trust that she'd be there for them, but she also understood that she'd broken it one too many times.

Tiki took her hands and squeezed. "I'm going to need both you and Tonya through this. Please don't break my heart this time."

Shit. That was a tough pill to swallow and there was nothing Tayla could say in her own defense, even though she had an entire speech forming in her brain. The words dropped to her tongue, but she refused to unleash them.

There was no point.

She'd made a promise to her grandfather and she wouldn't dare break it. She also told her sisters the earliest she'd leave would be Wednesday night or Thursday and that if all went well, she'd come back.

Those were promises she could keep.

Unless all hell broke loose, and then she'd be groveling. But she would be honest as to why, where in the past she'd sneak out, avoid, and give all the same excuses.

"I love you, Tiki," Tayla said. "I will have my cell with me at all times. Keep me posted." She waved her phone, taking a step back. She watched her sister pull out of the driveway and head off down the long windy road.

Fireflies filled the sky.

Tayla smiled.

As a child she used to love to run around, catching the funny creatures, putting them in a mason jar, and then she and her sisters would sit out on the dock and watch them light up as if they were the beam of light guiding vessels safely home.

She glanced over her shoulder. Through the

window, she could see Gael sitting in his family room with a glass of wine in one hand and a tablet in the other. He hadn't come over today. Not that he wasn't welcome. Her parents had invited him and she had even banged on his door and asked if he wanted to go waterskiing.

But he declined, stating he had things he needed to do before his brother-in-law came over for supper.

For a moment, she took it personally. As if *he* didn't want to spend time with *her*. But then he smiled, yanking her into his foyer and kissing her tenderly. It was a brief kiss. A stolen moment, but she cherished it.

And she wanted more.

She should be heading up to her room to check email, messages, and do a little work, but instead she strolled across the yard toward his front door. The pull to spend time with him didn't make sense. Just because they were compatible in the bedroom, didn't mean they were compatible anywhere else.

But he made her body tingle in ways she'd forgotten existed. That drove her crazy. Just because she didn't have time for romance, didn't mean she didn't allow herself the simple pleasure of sex.

Self-satisfaction was okay and did the trick every once in a while.

But after a few weeks, it wasn't enough. She needed the real thing. Examining that thought now, she realized how cold that made her seem. How she'd been using some of the people in her life. She paused about twenty feet from Gael's front porch.

There was something different about Gael and they had a connection. Take away the obvious attraction—and the mind-blowing sex—and they had deep bond that she couldn't explain.

Her feet moved across the path and the next thing she knew, she stood at the door. She raised her finger tentatively and pushed the doorbell. She reminded herself this wasn't about sex. It had nothing to do with her personal life and everything to do with her work life. Gael would help her come up with a work plan that made sense to her family. One that would give her everything she wanted.

One that provided the balance she needed so she wouldn't lose her sisters because she understood that's where this was headed.

But keep her career.

She had to have both.

The wood rattled and she searched her brain for

something to ask him, but nothing intelligent came to mind.

"Oh. Hi," he said with a smile.

"Hey," she said softly.

"What brings you by?" He stepped to the side and waved his hand toward the foyer.

The last time she'd been inside this house had to have been when she'd been in high school.

A lot had changed.

The hardwood floors had been completely replaced. They were now light in color and a wide plank. The cathedral ceilings had matching beams that spanned from one room to the next.

"I had walked my sister to her car and I saw the light on," she said.

"Would you like a glass of wine? I just opened a bottle of red. It's a nice blend."

"Sure. Thanks." She followed him into the other room. "I know the previous owners did some work, but wow, this place is amazing." She ran her fingers over the granite counter at the bar area in the family room.

"I bought it for three reasons. The first one being I didn't have to do a single thing to it besides furnishing the place." He handed her a glass before going back to his spot on the couch.

She stood awkwardly in the middle of the room for a long moment, deciding if she should sit next to him.

Or across from him.

She didn't want him to think she came over here for one reason, and one reason only.

She decided to live dangerously and joined him on the sofa. Raising her glass, she swirled her wine before taking a long, slow sip. She let the liquid settle in her mouth before swallowing. "Wow. That's good."

"It's my favorite and it's not cheap."

"Am I going to dislike my twelve-dollar bottle from now on?"

He laughed. "Oh yeah. That's not going to cut it anymore."

"Wonderful."

"Remind me before you leave tonight and I'll send you home with a couple of bottles." He rested his hand on her thigh.

She stared at his fingers dancing across her leg. "You don't have to do that."

"I don't mind. I buy it by the case. It's my one vice I brought back with me from the city." He laughed. "Okay. I have expensive taste and some of that has stuck with me, but since I'm not employed and I'm currently living off my savings, this is the only thing I indulge in."

She glanced around the house at all the brand-new furnishings. The paintings on the wall that didn't look as though they came from a cookie-cutter department store. She ran her fingers over the plush leather under her butt. "Are you kidding me? This place is filled with one-of-a-kind pieces and don't even get me started on the water toys."

"In my defense, I bought the boats and stuff to entice my brother-in-law to bring his boys."

"I'm dying to ask you the most inappropriate question on the planet."

"You want to know my shoe size?" He winked. "Oh, wait. You have firsthand working knowledge of that."

She felt a giggle bubble in her throat. "What are we? Twelve?"

"I'm a guy. We don't grow up," he said, lowering his chin and raising his glass. "Go ahead. Ask me anything."

Sometimes it was hard to figure him out. He could be incredibly serious at times, but he had a sarcastic flair to him that he inserted at moments where pensive would be more appropriate. What was even more confusing was when he mixed the two. She wasn't used to that. She could handle one or the other.

She reached up and fiddled with her messy bun. When she wore her hair in a ponytail at work, it was low, tight, and at the nape of her neck. And it was with a side part. Not this floppy thing with hair falling out of the scrunchie. Of course, every hair style had been based on what outfit she chose. Her closet consisted of a combination of her own handmade designs, carefully chosen designers that she knew Anna approved of, and of course Anna Declay Designs.

But Tayla never mixed and matched.

That would either get her fired or sent back to dressing mannequins.

Neither option was acceptable.

"It would be rude."

"But everyone who lives on this road and has gotten to know me wants to know how long I can live like this without working. Am I that rich?"

She laughed, reaching over her shoulder for her hair, only all of it was on top of her hair. She dropped her one hand to her lap and sighed. She raised her glass and sipped.

"Is that what you want to know?" he asked, pushing the subject.

"Kind of."

He shifted, resting his arm on the back side of the sofa, his fingers now dancing across the back of her neck, massaging gently. "I helped make money for some of the wealthiest people in this country. They paid me well and I used my skills as a financial advisor and invested. If I stay on a budget and if I stop buying things, I could stay unemployed for a few more years."

"Is that what you want to do?"

"I've decided I want to do two things," he said. "The first one is investing in a small business. Maybe a start-up. A creative one. Something that my sister would be proud of."

"What did you sister do?"

"She was an art teacher, but when she was younger, she dreamed of having her paintings hanging in art galleries. She did have two showings before following Greg to Albany and going back to school to get her teaching degree." He waved his hand toward the far wall. "Every piece of art you see hanging on my walls Piper did."

"Are you serious?" She jumped to her feet and raced across the room, holding her glass high so she didn't spill the wine. She examined the abstract piece with its bold colors. Bright reds and oranges with splashes of blue.

It was spectacular.

A true artist's works. Tayla might not be a painter, but she understood the profession. It wasn't all that different from being a designer. One had to comprehend colors, textures, and have a unique eye for detail on a level the average person didn't possess.

These paintings were done by someone who had a flair for being daring. Bold. Someone who wasn't afraid to push the envelope, but hadn't yet found their style.

She strolled to two smaller pieces on the wall by the stairs. "She was incredibly talented."

"I thought so."

Tayla glanced over her shoulder. "Why did she give up on her dream?"

"I asked her the same thing when she packed up her belongings and left the Big Apple." Gael rose and made his way to the bar. He refilled his glass and then brought the bottle to where she stood and poured her more wine. "Her response was that if I believed she gave up, then I hadn't been paying attention."

"That's not an answer."

Gael laughed. He turned and set the bottle back on the bar. "I agreed and pressed her to explain because for as long as I could remember, she wanted her paintings to hang in people's homes. She wanted to share her gift with the world. She sat me down and explained that her dreams had never been singular and that having a family had always been part of the equation. She'd fallen in love with Greg and it was time to readjust. She'd had two showings and while they got some attention, it wasn't enough to bring in the kind of buyers who would take her to the next level. She was content with where she landed and she could share her passion by teaching it. And that's what she did. It's why she and Greg chose to live in Saratoga. She taught high school there, but he works at Albany Medical."

"Wait a second." She leaned closer to one of the smaller paintings and studied the signature.

Piper.

That was it. No last name.

But that wasn't what struck her. "My boss has one of your sister's paintings hanging in her office. It's always been there. She said she bought it when she first came to the city from an up-and-coming artist as a reminder of where she was going."

"Piper's first show was fifteen years ago. She was

only twenty-three at the time. Her second one was six months later."

"Wow. She left that world really young."

"That's what I said and I thought she sold out by becoming a teacher and settling down so fast. What I didn't understand was how truly happy she'd been with her life choices and how utterly unhappy I'd been." He ran a hand across the top of his head. "Sometimes I wonder if I got married to prove to Piper that she could have had it all. Her career as an artist. A husband. Kids. Whatever she wanted, but she quit instead."

"You're married?" Her heart dropped to her gut and bounced to her throat like a basketball. That hadn't been anything she'd heard before.

"Divorced," he corrected.

"How long were you married?" Her brain filled with a million more questions.

"Four years. She left me because I loved my job more than I loved her and that is a true statement. I treated her like a piece of furniture."

"That's disgusting." Tayla narrowed her stare. The man she knew would never. He was kind and considerate. Loving even.

"Trust me. I know. I've apologized to Stacey, my ex-wife, and while she accepts it, she still has lingering issues from our marriage and I hate myself for that."

"What do you mean?"

"She told me that it would have been easier if I'd cheated on her because that she could understand. But the fact that I preferred to work instead of spending time with her didn't make sense. It made her feel less than and if I had been screwing someone else, she would have been able to tell herself that I was an asshole. Instead, she internalized everything and it made her feel as though she wasn't good enough. That she lacked something as a wife and I didn't want to be with her."

"Did you want to be with her?"

"I didn't love her the way a husband should, so no. I didn't. Not in the forever kind of way."

She made her way back to the couch and set her wine on the table. She leaned back, kicking off her flip-flops and tucking her feet under her butt. "But did you love her at all?"

"I did," Gael said. "I have a lot of regrets with Stacey. However, I wasn't willing to compromise when it came to almost everything in our marriage. I came home one day and she was gone and you know what I did?"

"No. What?"

"I opened a bottle of wine and went to bed. I didn't try to find her or call her or beg her to give me a second chance. I shrugged it off and went on with my life exactly like I'd always done."

"I'm sorry, but I kind of don't like that version of you."

"I kind of don't blame you." He leaned against the bar. "It's not one of my proudest moments and to be honest, when I look back on the last fifteen years of my life, I still feel a lot of shame."

"Oh. I'm sorry." She raced to his side and wrapped her arms around his waist. "I didn't mean to make you feel bad. I can see that you've changed."

"I'm a work in progress." He curled his fingers around her wrist and kissed her palm. "I always worry that I could become that man again if I'm not careful and sometimes I see a little bit of him in you."

She recoiled, taking a full step back. "What the hell is that supposed to mean?"

He took a healthy gulp of his wine and let out a long breath. His left eye twitched. "Did you read your old goal worksheets before sending them to me?"

"I didn't need to. I know what's in them. I understand myself. I know what I want and I resent you implying that I'm anything like the person you just described."

"First, I didn't say that. Second, are you doing this to placate your grandfather?"

"No." She shook her head. "I want to compare where I am now to what my goals were when I graduated and push out another five-year plan." She held up her hand. "I also know I need to make more time for family. My grandfather always told me that planning gives you that freedom."

"My brother-in-law is a huge believer in that. I call him the list guy. You walk into his house and he's got lists everywhere and I'm not talking a grocery list. I'm talking timestamped daily activity lists. He actually sends me calendar invites for everything. He's more organized than anyone I know."

"That's awesome." Tayla wished she had that skill. She tried and for a week or two, she'd been really good at it, and then she'd start slacking. But she never missed a deadline, so her system worked. "But nothing you've said so far explains how I'm like the person you described who was married to your ex-wife."

He glanced toward the ceiling and rubbed his chin with his thumb and forefinger in a contemplative gesture. "When Tiki accused you of not being there for her and how that made her feel as though work was more important than people."

Tayla opened her mouth but the only thing that came out was a noise that sounded like a dying chipmunk. She cleared her throat. "I know I screwed up. I don't need you telling me that. I'm doing what I need to in order to correct that and make adjustments so that never happens again."

"Okay. What about earlier today when you were sitting with your sisters by the water with your computer. What were you doing? Working?"

She sucked in a hot breath. It burned her lungs. The blood racing to her heart ignited into flames. How dare he judge her for checking and responding to email.

Or for doodling a little with her designs.

Being on the lake put her in a creative mood and she wanted to capture the moment. She could sketch and chat at the same time.

"You told me you needed to come over here so your family wouldn't hover while you took just a few hours out of the day instead of all day doing what I just witnessed."

"No." She shook her head. "I asked for space because my parents are constantly knocking on my door, asking if I need anything, pulling me from my focus. That way I can work for a few hours and not be late for dinner or whatever my family has planned when everyone else isn't working because it appears that I'm the only one who took a vacation." She pulled her hair from her bun and twisted a few strands between her fingers. "Besides. My sister was thumbing through a magazine while I was making tweaks to a finished design. Nothing that needed my full attention." She kept her tone even, making sure she didn't let her emotions run too hot. Her grandfather always told her when that happened, there was something to whoever pushed her buttons. "But I still needed to deal with it all before I settled into it tomorrow," she said. "I appreciate all your help with my goal worksheet and giving me a space to work. I even appreciate your candor. I'm sorry for your loss and everything that you're going through. However, I'm not you."

"I never said you were." He pushed from the counter and rested his hands on her shoulders.

"Yes, you did." She swallowed her breath. Gael put new meaning into the phrase *sex appeal*.

"What I meant was that there are moments when I look at you and the way you are with your sisters and I remember how close Piper and I used to be and I ignored the tightness in my chest as we grew apart. I chalked it up to being adults. To taking care of business. Where she knew that I was slowly becoming someone else. It would be one thing if that person was a better version. But it's not."

"Wow. I'm supposed to sit here and let you keep on insulting me."

"You're an amazing woman. Talented. Funny. Beautiful. I love spending time with you and I'm sorry that I suck at being tactful. I just don't want you to make the same mistake and I see you doing it." He pressed his hand against the center of his chest. "I feel it to my core and it's breaking my heart."

"That's dramatic."

"I know. I've never experienced this kind of emotion before and I'll be honest. I'm running a little scared." He fanned her face, running his thumb over her cheek. "I like you. I care about you." He kissed her softly. "I've studied your plans. You're not following your career goals. You might think you are, but you're not."

She opened her mouth but before the words that she couldn't take back tumbled out, her phone buzzed. Quickly, she checked it.

Tiki: *If you're up, I could use someone to talk to.*

"I promised my sister I'd be there for her

tonight." Tayla waved her cell. "Otherwise, you'd be getting a tongue-lashing like no other."

He groaned. Loudly. "I didn't take that the way you meant it." He dared to wink.

And she couldn't help it. She smiled while her insides turned to mush. "You make me nuts."

"The feeling is mutual," he whispered. "I wouldn't bother to say anything if I didn't like you and want you to have all your hopes and dreams come true. Whatever those real ones are and I want to help you explore them." His intense dark eyes held her captive. She couldn't move. Her feet were cemented to the floorboards.

His tongue peeked out between his lips and before she could even blink, they were on hers like a beef on weck. They were warm and tasted like the rich full-bodied wine they'd been drinking.

She certainly could get drunk on him without even trying.

The worst part was she should be pounding her fist against his shoulders and shoving him away because of the hurtful and untrue things he'd been saying. He'd known her for all of three days. Barely.

He knew shit.

And yet, there she was, twisting and twirling her tongue around his in a wild tango and loving every second of it and honestly, she couldn't wait to spend time with him tomorrow.

She had to admit, even if only to herself, she was curious about what he had to say about her past plans and how they weren't aligning with her current role. He was full of shit, but she'd give him the benefit of the doubt since he didn't understand the fashion industry.

The only problem was how could she keep from letting this happen again?

"I need to go," she managed as she broke off the kiss. "I'll see you at six?"

"I'll be ready." He led her to the front door. "I hope your sister is okay."

"Thanks." She smiled and then slipped outside and scurried across the yard, clutching her phone, her heart hammering between her ears.

Her sister might need her to be a sounding board about Josh, and she was happy to oblige. But Tayla was in over her head when it came to Gael.

It was like she jumped into the deep end with a damn brick tied to her feet.

8

Gael ruefully regretted his decision to let Tayla set the pace as he stared at her adorable ass in a pair of leggings that left nothing to the imagination. He took a gulp of his water. He'd done this hike at least two dozen times in his life. While it was a challenge, today it felt like the climb went on forever and his muscles ached.

"We're almost to the top." She glanced over her shoulder and smiled.

He was never going to make it through the day without touching her, like he'd promised himself.

The fact that she'd let him kiss her last night without slapping him had been nothing short of a miracle. Talk about opening mouth and inserting foot. The problem was he couldn't help himself.

The more time he spent with her, the more he wanted to lift her feet off the ground and shake her until she agreed she could do things a different way. That there were other paths to achieve her goals.

Different choices.

But he couldn't do that. It wasn't his place.

He wasn't the boyfriend.

He was barely a friend. Just because they had sex once didn't mean a damn fucking thing.

"I can see the end of the trail," she said.

"Good. Because I'm starving and those breakfast sandwiches your grandfather packed are making me crazy." He was hungry but it wasn't the smell of bacon or the fact that Maxwell had put them in some contraption that would keep them warm that was currently sending him on a tailspin.

She laughed. "When me and my sisters were little and we'd go on our adventures, he'd always make sure we were well fed. We were all lucky we didn't end up being like eight hundred pounds or something." She leaned forward, gripping a few of the rocks as the hike became slightly more challenging. "This gets me every time."

"Let me help." He stepped around her, climbing up in front and offering his hand.

"I've got it." She tested her foot on part of the

boulder. Another. She went back to the first one and hoisted herself forward. Unfortunately, she started to slide down. "Shit," she mumbled.

"Take my hand." He lunged, finding her wrist and yanking her up the rocky incline. He stumbled backward. Glancing over his shoulder, while holding her in his arms, he found a foothold.

She crashed into his chest. "Oh. Hello," she said breathlessly.

"Hi right back." He kissed her nose. It was impossible to ignore the pull she had over him and perhaps he shouldn't bother. "Are you okay?"

"I'm fine." She smoothed down the front of her leggings. "I forget how hard this part is."

"The first few times I hiked the mountain, we only went to what is referred to as second lookout, but this section right here is the hardest."

"I remember." She held his hand as he helped her maneuver over the last few rocky sections. The hike to the top was only a little over three miles. It took about two hours to get to the top, which he had to admit he was totally impressed by her pace. For a workaholic, she was totally in shape. "God. I love it up here," she said as they made the crest.

The view from the top of Buck Mountain brought back so many memories. The first time he'd climbed it all the way to the top he'd been ten. Piper had been so jealous because she wasn't old enough. She'd been forced to go on a rowboat hike to Phelps Island because of her age. Of course, boys and girls didn't do three-day hikes together.

Another bone of contention with Piper back in the day.

She'd been progressive and a feminist before she even knew what the words meant. Even when she'd settled into adulting and had her children, her mindset had been that boys and girls weren't all that different and she resented that they were treated differently.

Having been her brother, he had to admit that Piper could do anything he could do. He might have been taller. And maybe a little stronger.

But being a girl didn't mean Piper was less capable and she proved that time and again.

"Don't you love it up here?" She stood at the lookout with her hands on her hips and exhaled. "Tonya was always the hiker in the family and she would beat me and Tiki to the top by about fifteen minutes. We'd make her carry the bag with the food so she'd set up the picnic."

"Piper and I never hiked this mountain together," Gael admitted. "The camp at the base had opening ceremonies sometimes at first lookout, so we did that sort of together. We always said we'd do it, but it never materialized." Because of him. He pulled off his day pack and sat down at the picnic table. Being in this spot often brought up all the negative emotions that went with why he'd almost packed it in and went back to the city right before he'd bought the house.

Greg had been adamant that he'd never let the boys have a relationship with Gael, especially considering that Gael had only met Sam twice. The kid was four years old, and they only lived a few hours from each other, but Gael hadn't taken the time to get to know his family.

"Did you love going to Camp Mohican?" Tayla sat down across from him and opened her egg sandwich. "I imagine it was amazing."

"It was a lot of fun." He stared out over the lake below. The sun peeked out over the mountains and turned the sky a soft blue that matched the color of her eyes. "We looked forward to it every summer and my sister really wanted her boys to experience camping and all that."

"My dad's idea of camping is setting up a tent in the backyard. As a matter of fact, every summer, we'd pester him about taking the boat to the narrows or the mother bunch or even Long Island. And every year he'd say okay. Let's do it. We'd climb in the boat with our shit, and he'd drive around for a bit and then head home where Grandpa had set up a fake campsite. It was so stupid, but we started to make a game of it. Our own little Johnson adventure. One year the three of us wore pirate hats and pretended we were going on a treasure hunt. My dad drove the boat around for two hours. We even stopped at Glen Island and bought what we dubbed *special treasure hunting supplies*." She shook her head and let out a soft laugh.

Sometimes when she reminisced about her childhood her blue eyes sparkled like the ocean mist dancing under the light of the moon and the stars. It was incredible and he loved how animated she became. Her hands moved more. She wiggled in her seat. Her tone of voice went up an octave higher. She didn't speak any faster. No. She did that when she spoke about work, which was more of a nervous energy attitude. And then the color of her eyes dulled. Strained. Unhappy.

He wanted to find out why the thing that she believed she was passionate about, gave her stress.

"When we made it back to our house, Grandpa had set up a treasure hunt for us. We spent the whole weekend outside in the tent. We'd only go inside the house to use the bathroom."

"That is amazing," Gael said. "Sounds like your family has some vivid imaginations."

"Oh. We are a bunch of creatives. Even Tiki, the boring paralegal. You should hear her sing. She was in all the musicals in high school and in college. We have no idea why she went into the profession she did, other than the fact she had this weird obsession with the constitution and constitutional law, but didn't want to go to law school." Tayla spread out all the food. "One time Grandpa set up a whole murder mystery theme for us to solve on the camping trip."

"Who was the victim?"

"He was. We got to the dock and he was lying on it with a sign pinned to his chest. After we got to the platform to set up, he changed clothes and pretended to be a cop. It was too funny."

"Your family is amazing and creative. I love it." Gael was blown away by her stories and he took mental notes. These would be great things to play with the boys. He could only hope that she wouldn't mind if he stole a few of them and that Greg thought they would be fun too. "But I have to ask, why didn't your dad want to go on a real camping trip?" The old Gael wouldn't have been interested in the why. He wouldn't have cared. He would have actually been bored stiff by the personal story. He would have listened. Nodded his head and laughed appropriately. He would have taken the pieces that were important—if she were a client—so that he could impress her the next time they spoke. But he would have never been interested in what made her—or anyone else in her family—tick.

"It was something he used to do with his brother and for a long time, he just couldn't bring himself to do it. He wanted to. For us. However, he worried he'd be sad and that it would take away from our experience. We, of course, didn't know this at first. But when we found out, we made sure that our fake camping was better than the real thing. When we got older, he said we could take the boat ourselves, but we got so used to his way that we stuck with it."

"That's sweet. When was the last time you went on a fake camping trip?"

"When Tonya graduated from high school, I think."

"That was a few years ago," Gael said.

She tossed a piece of egg at him. "Thanks for the reminder that I'm getting old." She stuck her tongue out.

"Well, if it makes you feel any better, I'm a few

years older than you." He could sit here with her for hours. He hadn't enjoyed someone's company like this since—well, he had no idea. For years, life had literally passed him by. But he wasn't about to let that happen again.

And he didn't want to see it happen to someone as amazing as Tayla.

He needed to stop staring.

"Not really." She picked off a piece of her sandwich and plopped it in her mouth. Even the way she ate her food made him want to take her into his arms and kiss her wildly. He remembered when Piper first met Greg and how she would describe how he made her feel. How she couldn't concentrate on anything other than him and how he shaped the direction of her art. The way she viewed her work. Her world.

Her life.

Piper told him the moment she'd met Greg, everything that she thought she knew about herself shifted. Everything became clearer and she knew without a doubt that he was the one.

Well, Gael didn't know anything about his life with any certainty, except three things.

He wanted a relationship with Greg and the boys.

He didn't want to go back to the city or his old job.

And Tayla made his heart beat faster and since he'd met her, he hadn't been able to stop thinking about what it would be like to wake up with her in his bed.

Not for one morning either.

For a million mornings.

He coughed as he choked on his food.

And that thought.

No woman had ever affected him the way she had. Not even Stacey, and man, had she turned his head when they'd first met. They had passion in the bedroom.

At first.

But even that hadn't lasted very long.

"I have to be honest," he started. "I was a little worried you might not show this morning."

"Why?" She twisted off the cap of her water and chugged. Condensation dripped from the bottle to her lips.

He was in deep shit.

"I insulted you. And then I kissed you as if I had the right to."

She crumpled the foil and tossed it in the trash bag her grandfather had provided. "I'd like to make it very clear that I *allowed* you to kiss me. That I liked it and as for the first part of that statement, well, I forgive you."

"Thanks." He tossed and turned half the night, thinking about the things he'd said last night. His delivery could have been better, but he stood by his words. "Did you get a chance to look at your goal worksheets?"

"Unfortunately, I was up until midnight chatting with my sister, so the answer is no." She leaned forward, resting her elbows on the table. "But what is it specifically that has you believing that I'm not following the right path? And I really want to know. So don't worry about insulting me."

"Come on." He stood, holding out his hand. "It's going to take a good hour or so to get back down. Let's walk and talk."

"All right."

"First." He adjusted his backpack and took a chug of water before offering his hand.

She glared.

"What? You took it on the way up?"

"I got this," she said.

He raised his palms. "At least let me go first just in case." He headed down the rocky incline, some of which were loose. He moved as quickly as he could.

He worried she might slip and fall, potentially taking them both out.

The sound of rocks shifting caught his attention. He turned just in time to see her flap her arms as she slid down one of the larger rocks.

"Whoa." Her face contorted. "Shit. Ugh." She landed on her butt and grabbed her ankle. "That hurt." She leaned forward, resting her head on her knee and rocked back and forth.

He shrugged off the backpack and got down to her level. Her foot wasn't stuck. That was good. "Did anything snap?"

"No. I don't think I broke it. Just twisted it. Give me a second. I'll be okay." She shook out her hands and tilted her face toward the sky, scrunching her nose and pursing her lips like she'd sucked the juice of an entire lemon in one sitting. "Help me up."

He took her arm and lifted it over his shoulder. "Put all your weight on me at first."

Thankfully, she did as he asked. One thing he'd learned about Tayla was she was fiercely independent. Piper had been the same way. She didn't like being told what to do or how to do it. If anyone dared, beware. Greg had once tried to mansplain and he learned real quick that if he wanted to go the long haul with Piper, he better not ever do that again.

And he never did.

"Let's get you to a little flatter ground and see how that ankle holds up." He held her by the waist and carefully navigated the last few rocks. "Does it throb?"

"A little," she said. "I hate it when I do that. My ankles are so weak and I haven't gone hiking like this in years. These boots are old."

"Hold still. Let me look." He knelt, rolling up her legging. He cupped her ankle and gently squeezed. It didn't feel swollen. "Does this hurt?"

"It's sore."

"Hold on to my shoulders. Lift your leg and twist your foot around." He watched the motion of her leg, satisfied nothing was broken. "I'm going to find you a walking stick. I want you to use it, even on the flatter parts. And any rocky patch. You're going to use me and you're not going to argue about it." He stood and gave her his best *don't mess with me* look. The one his dad used to give him and Piper when he meant business.

She burst out laughing.

"I'm serious."

"Maybe but that face makes you look constipated."

"I'm going to pretend you didn't just say that." He turned and retrieved the backpack, securing it in place while he found her an appropriate stick. He handed it to her and watched as she tested it out. "How does it feel?"

"Better. I'll be fine."

"Let's take it slow, anyway." The trail from this point to the next lookout had two rocky sections. One that was relatively steep. After that, the only other part that would be tough was by the second lookout. The rest should be easy. "Are you sure your ankle is okay? I can carry you."

"It's still a bit sore, but really, it's going to be fine. Can we talk about my goals instead of my stupid weak ankles, please?" She took her stick and smacked his ass with it.

He groaned. If he chose to respond to the flirting, they'd never discuss her goals and get through a new plan. Of course, his imagination went right to mentally undressing her so he was fucked.

"If you can keep your stick off me, we can get down to business." The trail veered to the right and down some rocks. He wanted to give her a ride on his back, but instead, he offered his hand. They navigated the path together. He tested a rock, making sure it was stable, and she followed his footsteps. "Instead of me telling you why I think you've taken a different turn, I'd rather ask you a series of questions and all I ask is that you answer honestly. I don't want justifications as to why you're doing what you're doing. Don't give me a dissertation so that I will understand your choices. That's not what this exercise is about."

"Why do I get the feeling this is something that's done in some therapy retreat or something."

He chuckled. "It kind of is. Greg taught it to me and I'm using it to help guide myself through what it is that I really want to do with my life."

"And how's it working for you?"

"Honestly, I'd be lost without it. I know the direction I want my life to take."

"Oh, really. What's that?"

"Boy, are you good at avoiding," he said. "We can talk about me when we're not on limited time." He released her hand as the trail became flat and there were no more rocks. Not because he wanted to, but because if he didn't, he was going to need more than a cold shower.

"Fine. Start asking before I change my mind."

"Think back to your childhood. What is the first

memory that pops into your head about fashion? Don't overthink this question and don't go into detail. Be generic."

"Loving how fabric felt in my fingers when I went to the sewing store with my mom."

"How old were you?"

"Seven or eight," she said. "I loved all the different textures and colors. It was like a party for my senses. Even the smells were amazing. From that point on, I examined clothes. It started with my dolls, and then I got annoying and started taking apart my clothes. That made my mom crazy until I was able to put them back together properly."

"I imagine that might be obnoxious."

"I only really got in trouble when I ripped apart one of her dresses. It was one she never wore, so I didn't think anything of it. I wanted to try to create my own pattern."

"Were you successful?" He paused to wait for her to step over a few rocks.

"I was." She smiled proudly.

"How did that make you feel?" The whole point of this exercise was to bring her back to the beginning. To find her creation story. Everyone had one.

His had been his love for math and solving problems. His sister used to call him an oxymoron. By definition, he was a nerd.

But he wasn't because he hung out with the popular crowd and he was a bit of a jock. He didn't make sense, according to Piper. However, he didn't care. His peers sometimes made fun of him because he belonged to the math and chess club. He loved making fake money with his stock portfolio. But the moment he had that feeling where everything came together was when he helped a college professor with his start-up. It had been the right investment at the right time and it paid off for both of them.

That company was thriving today and Gael was proud he'd been in on the ground floor. It wasn't bringing in millions for Gael. Far from it, but it was what dreams were made from.

"Like I'd done the impossible."

His pulse increased. That was the sweet spot.

"What was your first job in fashion? After you graduated with your degree."

She laughed. "I dressed mannequins. It's like a rite of passage for all designers."

"Did you like it?"

"Actually, it was kind of fun."

"How so?"

"For starters, I got to play with accessories.

Dress up the clothing with a purse or a scarf. I got to add a little bit of flair to things. A touch of my style without being intrusive to the designer. Window displays were the best. Especially when I was assigned a holiday one or even better, one for a special showing," she said. "It also got me my next job working fashion shows. Some thought it was a step down, but for me it was all about learning the business. This gave me the opportunity to work the runway. I was dressing models, making sure they had the right pieces and all the good stuff."

"When you worked fashion shows, was that for a designer?" He held out his hand as they approached another tricky section, but this time she batted his hand away.

"No. I worked for a company that oversaw the major events. I was able to meet and mingle with so many different people in the industry. Specifically, my friend Matthew, who introduced me to someone who worked at Harraha." She limped down the trail, scrunching her face.

Stubborn was about the only way to describe her right now.

"What's that?" he asked.

"Another designer and the last place I worked

before I got the job as an associate designer with Anna Declay Designs."

"What did you do for Harraha?"

"I was an entry-level designer."

"What is that?" he asked.

"I attended fashion shows, took notes, helped select fabrics, collaborated on sketches. Whatever I was asked to do, I did."

"You don't sound like you enjoyed it as much."

"I didn't." She sighed. "I don't understand why this history intake is important to my goals. You haven't even asked me what it is I want out of my career."

"That's not what this exercise is about." He handed her the water bottle. "Right now, we're examining the path that got you to this point, and that leads me to my next question which is, what was next?"

"That's easy. I ran into Matthew and I told him how much I hated working for Harraha. He suggested I come interview for Anna, so I did and I got the job as an associate designer. It wasn't much different at first, but then I got my first big break with Anna. It was a random right place, right time kind of thing. One of the other designers had screwed up and I happened to be standing there.

She asked me to take over the task, so I did. From there, she'd come find me and have me do things for her. Sometimes they were fashion related. Other times they were as stupid as picking up her dry cleaning."

"So, she was seeing how dedicated to her you could be."

"No," Tayla said with some anger and frustration laced on the single word. "Why does everyone think that?"

"Because I've been on both sides of that fence."

"I'm not sure I know what that means."

"I had a boss who asked all of us to do random weird shit in between the real stuff. It was all about who was willing to do whatever it took to get the promotion. I knew that. So I did it. When I was the boss, I did the same thing. The only problem is that sometimes, there was no job to be had. It was all about power and who had it. Not about moving up the ladder."

"Well, Anna has been saying for three years she wants to find a designer to pull from her ranks. She's come close twice before me."

"That's what I've heard." Gael moved to the side of the trail, letting some other hikers move past them as they made their way past the first lookout.

Besides, he figured she could use a bit of a break. "Do you trust Anna will give you a line with your name on it?"

"Yes and no," she said. "I'd be a fool to think she's going to hand me the keys to the kingdom. But I do believe one hundred percent she wants to pay it forward. But she wants one hundred percent loyalty to her and her brand. She wants you to completely fit into her vision."

"Piper and I used to have this argument about whether or not I could be creative. She used to laugh in my face when I said I was. She didn't believe a numbers guy had a creative bone in his body and I certainly didn't understand what made her paintings good, bad, or brilliant, but I often had to get creative with financial portfolios."

"I have to agree with your sister, that's so not the same thing."

"Maybe not, but my point is I didn't always stick with the formula and that's how I got noticed. You're being asked to stick with her brand. Do it her way. Is that really how you stand out above the rest?"

"That's how I do it in her wheelhouse. She doesn't reward people going against the grain. Only people who do things her way."

The trail opened out into what the camp called

the Intermediate Unit. It was where young boys from the ages of six to ten lived during the summer. The kids were still in school, so the only people at camp currently were a few full-time employees and volunteers working on putting a few fixes on cabins and other structures that might have suffered some damages during the harsh winter months.

Tayla waggled her index finger. "However, she's having me work on some original stuff, with her direction, for this private showing. That's why this is so important. It is my chance."

This is where Gael worried the most about Anna Declay's business practices. Or Anna in general. "What happened to the last person whom Anna tried to break out?" Gael arched a brow. He didn't need an answer since they'd already discussed it.

However, he did want to see her reaction to it.

"I'm not them," Tayla said.

"Okay. Tell me what makes you different." He glanced around at the cabins and it was hard not to think about his sister. He remembered all the times they chased each other around these very grounds. If he concentrated, he could almost hear her laughter.

But he wasn't here to deal with his pain.

This was about Tayla and helping her find the

balance in her life that he hadn't been able to before it was too late.

"The designer before me, I knew. I watched it happen and she got cocky. She truly believed Anna liked her as a person. That they were friends because Anna was being nice to her and treating her differently. I know Anna doesn't give a shit about me as a human. She only cares about what I can do for her and her company."

"I'm glad you accept she's got a knife ready to stab you in the back."

Tayla laughed. "I know this business can be cutthroat. Especially at this level. But it doesn't have to be like this forever. Once she puts my name on a line, I'll have more control. Other people will know me. I won't be a cog in the machine."

Boy, did he understand that thinking and if she was willing to completely sell her soul to the devil, have no life and no friends, she was right. It would change. She'd get to the top of her industry where she would be the one calling the shots. But she wouldn't recognize herself anymore.

The worst part was that if it happened, her heart would never be the same. That's what scared him about his life and why he worried so much about doing anything in the financial world. Even going into the city affected him in ways he couldn't explain. It was like he became a completely different person. Even his blood flowed in his body differently. It was fast and furious.

And hot.

Where today, right now, it ran hot because he was with Tayla. But it was more of an excited kind of heat. And while his heart beat a little faster, it was the kind of adrenaline that he would try to repeat over and over again, but couldn't because it was a falsehood.

This was real.

It wasn't a chase. It was life happening. In real time.

He still enjoyed an adrenaline rush. But instead of seeking it as a way of life, he did so in sailing. Or on a hike. He found what Greg called more appropriate ways to get that fix in.

Greg even made the suggestion that if he had to go jump out of a perfectly good airplane to keep from going back to being his old self, then he should do it.

However, Gael wanted to learn to live on a more even keel.

"Are you sure about that?" He paused at the front

of the girls' unit, opening the water bottle and taking a swig. He offered it to Tayla.

She shook her head. "Everyone has to start somewhere. Every designer worked under someone else. I pay my dues with Anna, and then I go out on my own."

"What's your exit strategy?" He sat on the bench that he'd once had his first kiss on. He'd been all of fourteen. The object of his affection had been the same age and one of the most popular girls at camp. Piper had been pissed because she didn't like the girl and well, the girl hadn't cared too much for Piper either.

The romance lasted about as long as the kiss.

These last few months had been one long trip down memory lane and there were times he hated every second of it. However, there were moments that he enjoyed.

Like this one.

Tayla joined him, stretching out her leg.

He lifted it, wanting to check out how badly swollen her ankle was. He noticed her limp had been getting better, but he also suspected she was the kind of person who didn't complain and didn't want him to know if she was suffering. He ran his hand over her calf and down. He frowned.

Swollen.

She winced but didn't jerk her leg. She needed ice and she probably shouldn't be walking on it at all.

"I hand in my resignation when I'm ready to be on my own," she said, staring off in the other direction.

"What is the criteria for that?" He ran his hand up and down her shin, careful not to put any pressure on her ankle. "Is it a timeline? A number of designs? Money? What?"

"It's when I have enough of my own personal collection and when I feel like I can leave." She turned, catching his gaze. "Once I get Anna to name me as her protégé and put my name on a line of my own, I know she's going to own my ass even more than she does now. I'm going to have to work longer and harder than I've ever had to before in the beginning." She adjusted her ponytail. "What I really need to do is factor in how to make more time for family and how to finish my own line for when I do leave Anna."

"That's an interesting dilemma," he said. "Why is it that you believe you need Anna to go out on your own? Why can't you do it now?"

"Because I'm no one in the fashion industry. I

wouldn't be able to get anyone to invest in me and I don't have the money. I'm saving a ton right now and getting a line with Anna would be more. But that's only one problem. Not being a name in this business, I wouldn't be able to get my designs in fashion week, or even smaller fashion shows without having some clout. I need to be bigger before I can step away."

"I'm sorry, but I don't buy that."

She opened her mouth. He pressed his finger against her plump, kissable lips.

"It's not for you to buy. It's for you to help." She wrapped her fingers around his wrist. "I hate to admit it, but this stupid twenty question game worked in the sense that I realized moving forward I need to plan for balance. I want to be able to protect my career and have a life." She squeezed his hands. "I don't want to cause my family pain. Nor do I want to give up my hopes and dreams."

"You act like it's all or nothing." He lifted her to his lap. "I might not know much about your world, but I know there are a lot of designers. Just like with Piper. She didn't need to become the top one percent where the pressure to stay at the top meant giving up your right arm, left leg, and your firstborn."

"You're being dramatic."

"Maybe a little," he said. "While I understand all the hurdles you have to jump over to get to the end result, I want you to at least look at the possibility that you can achieve your goal of being a designer with your own line without Anna Declay Designs."

"You don't get it," she said with a quivering lower lip. Her sweet blue eyes welled with tears.

He held her tight. "Why are you on the verge of tears?"

"The two other designers before me, she crucified their careers. They won't ever work in this industry again. They have been blackballed. She'll crush me if I walk away right now. She'll destroy my name. I have to pick the right time. And that will either be when one of three things happen. Someone turns her head before she gives me a chance. I design something she absolutely hates. Or she names me and puts me in a corner to do my thing while she starts dangling carrots in front of others because she kind of gets off on that."

He fanned her face. "I get it now. You feel trapped."

"I wouldn't go that far," she whispered.

"I would." He tilted her chin, licking his lips. "I have an idea."

"Should I be scared to hear it?"

"Probably," he whispered. All he wanted to do was kiss her, but he should get this out first. "I understand how important it is to you to develop your own line. Label. Brand. The whole thing. I also get you believe that since you've gone down this road with Anna, it's the only one. You've invested too much time and you've watched her be vindictive. You're frightened."

"Maybe a little."

"I want to work through this goal sheet your grandfather has made with Anna as the vessel, and then I want to do it with me as the vessel." Before she could protest and he'd have to explain an idea that he hadn't fully developed, he cupped the back of her neck and pressed his mouth over her lips.

She tasted like the morning dew on a cool spring morning.

He wrapped his arms around her waist, drawing her close to his chest.

Her fingers dug into his shoulders. "You need to explain what that means."

"I can't until I see your final goal sheet." He helped her to her feet. "You only have so many hours your family is going to let you work, so let's get you back to my place."

She groaned. "I kind of want to play hooky."

"We can do that too." He laughed. "I've got nowhere to go today." He laced his fingers through hers. Slowly, he led her toward the public parking area. "I've taken a liking to you."

"So your lips keep telling me," she said. "But getting romantically involved with you even temporarily would be an inconvenient complication."

9

Tayla carried the bottle of wine down to the dock. She'd been icing her ankle on and off and for the most part, it felt better, but it wasn't one hundred percent. Hopefully, in a few days, it would be as long as she didn't do any more major hiking.

That should be easy. No more major excursions with Gael. However, she would still be spending a fair amount of time with him and that posed a different set of problems.

She glanced over her shoulder.

Gael's lights were on, so she knew he was home, but she hadn't seen him since she stepped out of his den at three in the afternoon.

Two hours over her allotted time.

He hadn't given her too much shit for getting lost in her creative process. Only she hadn't been lost in her designs.

She'd been lost in her thoughts of him and all the things he made her think about. It had become difficult to concentrate on the designs Anna had expressed she wanted for the private showing. Guy Contra could be insanely particular. And he was notorious for changing his mind, even after he expressly stated what he'd been looking for.

He made Anna's demands seem almost simple and easy.

Tayla had been instructed by Anna to create ten pieces specifically for Guy's Manhattan store. These were to be one-of-a-kind outfits for the professional woman.

The concept didn't exist, which is what intrigued both Anna and Tayla. Working women, while most wanted to look their best, didn't dress in unique pieces that you couldn't find anyone else wearing.

Not unless you were a Kardashian.

Professional women didn't want to look overstated. They wanted to be noticed. Remembered. But not memorable. That had more of a negative connotation.

Tayla's designs needed to complement the

working woman, making her look successful, without being too sheik.

But creating a business line wasn't difficult, unless you were doing it for Guy Contra.

"What is taking you so long?" Tonya yelled. "Is that ankle still bothering you?"

"Just a little." Tayla picked up her pace. She'd managed not to be late for dinner and she promised her sisters an after-dinner beverage on the water.

Just the three of them.

No one else.

Which meant she needed to push all these thoughts to the back of her mind. They had no place swimming around in her brain while she spent time with her sisters.

Tomorrow she could tackle them.

She had all day.

Her parents were going into town. Her grandfather was going with them. She had their blessing to work.

Thank God.

Because she was now a day behind.

"Here you go." She handed the bottle to Tiki, who poured three very generous rounds. "So, who wants to hear about my day?"

"Are we going to have to listen about Josh?" Tonya asked.

Tiki sighed. "Yes."

"Why are you continuing to engage with him?" Tayla asked. "Unless you plan on taking him back, which we believe is a mistake."

"The thing is he told me about the affair. Who does that unless they are remorseful?" Tiki wrapped herself in a blanket.

Tayla sprawled out on one of the chaise lounge chairs. She tucked her hair behind her ears and crossed her ankles, making sure she had a good view of Gael's yard.

No sign of him.

Not yet anyway.

But she'd told herself that she wouldn't go over there. Not tonight. They were meeting in the morning to discuss her goal worksheet before she locked herself in his den. She had to finish those designs.

Her career depended on it.

"He can regret his actions all he wants. It doesn't mean he won't repeat it," Tayla said. "Besides, isn't he putting pressure on you to get married?"

"Yes. But we were talking about that anyway."

Tiki held up her hand. "I'm not agreeing to getting engaged. But I still love him. I can't turn that off."

"No one is asking you to," Tonya said. "However, you need to spend some time being your own woman."

"I agree. Take a month. Hell, take the summer to figure out who you are without him. Do all the things that he never would with you and then see how you feel." Tayla's cell buzzed.

Her body tensed. She had to look at it.

Matthew: *OMG. Girl. I don't mean to freak you out, but Grace just left Anna's office. I have no idea if it's good or bad. Her face was expressionless. Anna left fifteen minutes later. As in left the building. I doubt she'll be back. I'm doing some digging to find out what's going on. Call me if you need me.*

"Shit," Tayla mumbled.

"What's wrong?" Tiki asked.

"If I tell you, then you'll get mad."

"Work related?" Tonya lowered her head.

Tayla nodded.

"Go ahead. Deal with it." Tiki waved her hand. "You've been doing your best to be present. Just don't go racing off to the city. That would be unforgivable."

"Thanks. And I won't. Not tonight anyway." She

hopped to her feet and groaned as a dull ache shot from her ankle to her brain. She hobbled to the end of the dock where she tapped on Matthew's contact information. He answered before it rang.

"Girl. You didn't have to call."

"Yes. I did," she said. "Could you get any kind of read on either one of them?"

"No. And I don't know how Grace ended up in her office to begin with. I was asked to go help with the display for the Rubio showing. I don't know why, but my expertise was needed."

"Don't take this the wrong way, but was it really?"

"Oh, girl. Don't go disrespecting my reputation," Matthew said. "But no. Not really. At least not by the time I got there."

"And you don't find that suspicious when Grace was also working on that showing?" Tayla strolled up the path to the fire pit. She plopped herself down in the Adirondack chair.

"If it had been Grace asking me, I might have. But it came directly from Anna. I do not question the boss and I wasn't the only one she asked," Matthew said. "Another reason you don't need to worry about that part being sabotage. I was in the middle of something else and asked Anna if I could finish before heading down. She told me to get there when I could."

"I suppose that makes me feel a little better," Tayla said. "What happened next?"

"After the showing was put together properly, I headed back up to the design room where I saw Grace stepping from Anna's office. I rubbed my eyes to make sure they weren't playing tricks on me. But sure enough, that bitch strolled right on by me and into her tiny, sad, pathetic cubicle where she sat at her desk, texting, and then she left for the day."

"And you said Anna left shortly after?" Tayla was getting no new information and all this did was feed her insecurities. That was the last thing she needed.

"Anna went into her office and made a phone call. I don't know who to, but she laughed and sounded like she was having a fun conversation before she waved goodbye to me."

"Matthew, something is off with that. It's contrived. It feels like Anna is up to something and I don't trust that Grace doesn't have a hand in it."

"Give me the night to figure out what's going on."

"Shit. I promised my family I wouldn't leave until Wednesday night or very early Thursday."

"We still might be able to hold that schedule,"

Matthew said. "If Anna kept her word and told Guy your name, you are golden, sister."

"Yeah, but can we trust Anna to keep her word?" Tayla lifted her gaze as her two sisters came flying up the path. "Hang on, Matthew." She set her cell on her lap. "What's going on?"

"Foster just called me," Tonya said. "His ex-wife is in the hospital. She had an overdose. We're going to go sit with him. Do you want to come?"

Tayla blew out a puff of air. "Are you okay if I don't? There is a situation at work and if Gael is still awake, I want to ask his advice. I swear it's not—"

"It's okay." Tiki squeezed her shoulder. "This time we get it. We'll see you later."

She nodded. "I love you both."

"Right back at you." Tonya nodded.

"Okay. I'm back." She lifted her cell, pressing it to her ear.

"While you were gone, I did find out one thing, and it's not great."

Tayla sat up taller, bracing herself for impact. "That was fast."

"Well, I'm still at the office and I logged into Anna's calendar."

"How the hell do you have access to that?" she asked.

"I have access to a lot of things around this place," Matthew said. "There's a private meeting scheduled for Friday."

"I know. That's when I have my meeting with Guy."

"No. There are two meetings now. Both with a special client."

"Oh fuck," Tayla whispered. "She's been playing me this entire time."

"Not necessarily," Matthew said. "We don't know who the players are at this meeting. We don't even know for sure that both are meetings with Guy. It could be someone entirely different. Anna has a lot of different things going on right now, like the maternity line and the wedding line."

"But we know who's designing those. We know who will be in those meetings," she said.

"Do we? Because it's Anna we're talking about."

Tayla tapped her fingers on the wood armrests. Matthew had a point. Anna had scheduled design meetings and when everyone walked into the room, it wasn't what they expected. One time, Tayla thought she was going to be working with a group of junior associates on the spring collection when it turned out all she was expected to do was accessorize the showroom.

That was an entirely different task.

And a downgrade from what had been on the agenda.

At the end of the day, Tayla sucked it up and did the work, which won her a few brownie points with Anna because that's one thing that Anna admired more than anything else.

Hard work without question.

Loyalty.

Anna would almost always reward those two things. It was the almost always part that would crush a career.

"I should come back in the morning," Tayla said.

"You don't want to hear this, but if Anna is going to fuck you, coming back is going to let her do it sooner and in front of an audience."

"Anna sent me away. She told me to take this vacation." Tayla closed her eyes, remembering how giddy Anna had been over the prospect of being able to take one. It had all been a setup. "If I had stayed, she wouldn't have given this opportunity to anyone else."

"Girl. You don't know that."

"Matthew. We both know I'm right."

"Okay. So maybe you have a point," Matthew said. "But coming back before Thursday is going to show you running scared. It's also going to tip your hand that you know something is up, which I doubt will work in your favor. You should stay right where you are, work on your designs, which are fabulous, and come back just in time for your presentation. Obviously, she's pitting two designers against each other. Let the better woman win. We both know it's going to be you."

"I wish I had your confidence."

"Sister. You have to start believing in yourself. If you don't, no one else will. Besides, this isn't your only shot. There will be other opportunities if this doesn't work out."

She wasn't going to argue with Matthew. He didn't have to worry about Anna crushing his dreams with the blink of an eye. Nope. He wasn't a designer. He worked as an assistant to many up-and-coming fashionistas. He was what helped make stars. If it weren't for him, she'd be no one.

Something she was well aware of and if she went on to another designer or started her own line, she'd beg him to come with her. He might not. Matthew went wherever the wind took him and he'd whispered in her ear that he had three job offers last week, one definitely worth considering.

Matthew was lucky. The work he loved doing,

while so important, didn't require being noticed by the top dog the same as it did for someone like Tayla.

"I do believe in myself, Matthew. That's why I've been putting up with this bullshit from Anna."

"Oh, baby girl. You can tell yourself that all you want. But the truth of the matter is you haven't believed you could do it since I've known you. That's why you hide in places like Anna Declay Designs. But worse, you're letting it kill your creativity."

"Excuse me. What the hell is that supposed to mean?" She rubbed her temples. This wasn't the first time Matthew had mentioned that her work lacked some luster. Or as he put it, *the Tayla touch*.

"You know exactly what I'm talking about," Matthew said. "You're turning into this machine where all you do is crank out one line after the other that looks exactly like what everyone else in this place is doing. I told you that Anna plucked you from obscurity because you were better than her and everyone else in here and your dress got noticed. She needed you to keep her name on top."

"Are you telling me you don't trust she's going to break me out?"

"The private showing is lined up with a legit customer," Matthew said. "I believe she's giving you an opportunity to showcase your talent to a buyer. How that will play out, I don't know because Anna has never taken her little game this far before, with the exception of maybe Molly, but that wasn't—"

"That's so different."

"Is it? Because Molly was tasked with creating a line to show Anna under the pretense if it was good enough, and the creative team thought so, she'd take it to a buyer. Instead, Anna humiliated Molly in front of all of us and Molly hasn't worked in the fashion industry since."

"I don't need to be reminded about what happened to Molly." Tayla remembered the day like it was yesterday. Molly had been all abuzz about the collection she'd been working on for Anna. Her own designs. No directions from Anna. No cookie-cutter patterns. No limitations with fabric.

Molly got to do what she'd been passionate about and develop a ten-piece collection with a theme that made Molly's skin tingle. She'd been given free rein to do whatever she wanted. She'd been so proud that day that Tayla didn't think anyone could strip that smile off her face. Molly marched herself into that conference room like she owned it.

What Molly failed to understand was that had

been a test and the passing response would have been to keep her ego in check and find out exactly what Anna had been looking for. To ask probing questions, without being annoying. To create a line that Anna would be willing to put her name on and maybe give credit that she had help. All that meant was that the designs had a slight difference. That they veered off just a tad from what Anna had done the season before.

The reality was that Molly was a talented designer and that threatened Anna, so Anna had to find a way to either make sure Molly toed the line or left, but hopefully not for greener pastures and preferably with the understanding that Anna would destroy her if she ever tried to upstage her in her own house.

It was fucking exhausting and Molly learned the hard way when her designs were unique and flipping fabulous—and presented in a company setting, to company executives, for company clients—therefore owned by Anna Declay Designs.

Molly left that day defeated after she was told her creations weren't what Anna had been looking for. That Molly had gone completely off the deep end. Anna even took the sketches to the main board in the common room and ripped them apart in front of everyone. She explained to every designer who worked for her why Molly's designs would never become part of a collection—for any designer. It had been humiliating for Molly to have her hard work decimated like that.

The worst part had been when her new line was uncovered two months later and two of Molly's designs—while they had been altered some—were showcased as Anna Declay originals.

Molly had no recourse. Any work created for Anna, belonged to Anna. They all signed that contract.

Same went for Tayla. These designs. Once she handed them in, Anna owned them.

"Am I crazy to want to let it play out?" she asked, pinching the bridge of her nose.

"Girl. You're not crazy," Matthew said. "You're super aware of what Anna can do. We've done our best to factor that in. I just feel bad because I'm the one who told you about this job."

"Don't feel bad. You warned me from day one. I knew what I was getting into. This has always been a means to an end. If Guy Contra likes my designs, then I've been seen by someone else. She can't take that away from me."

"No. She can't," Matthew said. "But she has to actually put it in front of him."

Her heart dropped to her stomach like a penny falling from the top of the Empire State Building. You'd think it couldn't do a whole lot of damage.

But it's deadly.

"Any chance we can find out if he actually does have an appointment on Friday?"

"That's going to be almost impossible to find out for sure," Matthew said. "He keeps information about meetings with designers locked up tighter than Fort Knox. He doesn't want anyone to know who and what he's going to be carrying in his stores come the next season. He likes to make a big splash with those unveilings."

"I know. But people talk. Assistants gossip."

Matthew sighed. "I'll see what I can find out, but I'm telling you, he makes all those appointments himself. Only once did that intel leak and when it did, Guy canceled it and never bought from that designer again."

"I'm screwed," she whispered.

"No. You're not. You're going to make an awesome collection and you're going to bring it here on Friday. You're going to show it to Anna and hopefully Guy—"

"What if Guy's not there? What if you're right? What if this is similar to what happened to Molly and she does to me—"

"You're not Molly."

"I took a fucking vacation, Matthew. That's cocky. That's acting as if I believe I'm a cut above the rest. I did exactly what I knew I shouldn't and now Anna's going to destroy my career."

"She didn't destroy Molly's. That girl walked away from the business."

"And who was going to hire her after the shit Anna said publicly? Come on, Matthew. Don't sugarcoat things with me. This is either going to go really good or really bad. And let's face it, the likelihood the former is going to happen is slim," she said. "I'll be in the office by noon."

"No. You will not," Matthew said. "You will stay right where you are until Friday morning. I can't poke around in certain places if you're here. Just keep working and we'll figure it out and come up with a plan."

"I don't know."

"Trust me."

"All right. I guess it's not going to make a difference. I mean, if I come back now, she could just humiliate me faster," Tayla said.

"That's one way to look at it." Matthew had the audacity to chuckle. "Sweetie. I adore you. I've got your back. I'll check in with you in the morning. Night. Night."

"Good night." She sighed, setting her cell on her thigh. She glanced between her childhood home and Gael's.

Her sisters were gone for the night. Between dealing with Foster and the fact they both had to work in the morning, they wouldn't be returning. Her parents had most likely turned in for the night.

Gael's family room light was on, as well as his front porch. He was awake and she could use someone to talk to.

At least that was the excuse she gave herself when she rose to a standing position, tucked her phone in her back pocket, and made the decision to stroll across the yards.

Her heart beat so fast it hurt. She raised her hand and knocked three times. Immediately, she heard his feet stomp across the wood floors.

She swallowed her breath, wondering if this pure excitement of seeing him would ever go away. It seemed juvenile and yet she welcomed the sensation.

The door swung open and he stood on the other side.

"We've got to stop meeting like this," he said with a big smile and a glass of wine. "The neighbors might start talking."

She took the glass from his hand and took a hearty gulp. "God, I needed that."

"I'm insulted."

She turned and leaned into him, curling her free hand around his thick neck and rising up on tiptoe. She tilted her head and pressed her mouth against his, slipping her tongue between his lips in search of his. When she found it, she swirled and twisted hers around it in a wild, familiar dance with a new flair.

Desperation.

His arm came around her waist.

A guttural moan filled her throat.

"As much as I loved that and want more," he whispered, dropping his forehead to hers. "I need to know what's driving it because I taste more than your desire to be with me. I don't mind being there for you, even in the bedroom, but I need to know why you need me that way."

"That's fair." She inhaled his rich masculine scent. He smelled like a combination of pine and fresh spring water. It was intoxicating. "Can I have my own glass of wine?"

"Of course." He kissed her forehead, taking his glass. "What's wrong?"

She followed him into the family room and leaned against the bar. "Anna's going to screw me over."

"You know this for a fact?" He handed her a full glass of his favorite red blend.

She closed her eyes and took another long, slow sip, letting the full-bodied wine tickle her taste buds before hitting her gut with its full power. She blinked. "No. But after speaking with Matthew, it's the same pattern we've seen and the fact that I took this vacation was a setup. I can't believe I fell for it."

"What are you going to do?"

"Matthew talked me into waiting it out. Playing along, at least for now. He's going to take tomorrow and maybe the next day and see what he can find out about what Anna might really be up to."

"That actually sounds like a decent plan, but that doesn't mean you can't come up with one of your own." He set his glass down and folded his arms across his chest. "If I understand all this correctly, you're now concerned she'll destroy your name before you can even get your name out there, steal your designs, and you won't ever work again."

"Something like that."

"So, you might be mad at me, but I've done some research on your boss and she's pretty heartless from what I can tell."

"You did what now?" Tayla jerked her head and glared. She shouldn't be pissed. She brought Gael into this and had asked for his advice on her goal worksheet. That meant understanding a little bit about her current situation.

But never in a million years did she think he would go poking around her world without her knowledge.

"She reminds me a lot of my old boss. Always promising the keys to the kingdom, only never even opening the door a crack to let you see what he was really offering, and constantly fucking people over for his own personal pleasure. He did it to me so many times. The way he did is very different than in your business because he needed us to stick around. We each had clients. Rich ones. And he needed our portfolios because if I left, there might be some clients who were loyal to me. Not to the company. So, he'd wrangle a big fish. Dangle it in front of me, saying that client could be mine. Only, when it came down to it, he'd always keep them for himself, stating either the client wanted it that way or there was something wrong in my pitch or I had too much on my plate, whatever. There was always a reason that I didn't get the biggest fish."

"That does sound kind of familiar."

"You're not trapped," Gael said. "But I need to see your employment contract. And I need you to be open to my ideas."

"I can do both." She took in a deep breath and let it out slowly. "I'm tired of this game. I want off the roller coaster. But I don't want out of the game." She stared at him with tears burning in her eyes. "Does that make any sense?"

He took the glass from her hand and set it down, lifting her chin with his thumb and forefinger. "One of my biggest regrets in life—outside of not spending enough time with my family—is not being able to see how I lost my dream in the chase."

"I don't want to lose that. I just don't know what to do next."

"I think you need to sleep on it." He took her by the hand. "We can go over everything fresh in the morning."

"I don't want to go back to my parents'."

He smiled. "I wasn't suggesting you do."

"If I stay, nothing's changed. This is still temporary. My life, even if I don't work for Anna Declay Designs, is still in the fashion world and that's not here."

"I'm aware," he said. "I'm only hoping you choose not to sneak out until the crack of dawn."

Her mouth tugged into a smile. "My grandfather will be relentless in his teasing if he finds out and my dad will get great enjoyment out of trying to embarrass you."

"I'm a big boy. I can take it." He pulled her toward the stairs. "Why, just today your mom asked me three times if I enjoyed my hike and then wanted to know if all we did was work this afternoon."

"She's a piece of work."

"She loves you," he said at the stairs. His bedroom was at the end of the hall.

She noted that two of the rooms on the way there were decorated for little boys. That was sweet.

The other two guest rooms were decorated in the same style as the rest of the house and also had his sister's paintings. The nice part was that this home didn't feel like a shrine.

More like a dedication. His way to honor his sister.

"Did you pay for all these?" She ran her finger across the painting in the hallway.

"These are the ones that never made a showing or gallery," Gael said. "I've begged Greg to let me contact Piper's old friends in New York City, but he feels that would profiting in her death and he won't allow it. So they hang on my walls and his and a few we donated to the kids' school."

"That's sweet." She stepped into the master and Gael pulled her into his arms, kissing her passionately.

There was no mistaking his intent.

She melted into his body. Everything about him was strong and powerful. She felt safe in his embrace. Cared for.

But there was something stronger brewing between her and Gael. Something she couldn't deny.

Nor did she want to.

However, her career was still in New York City.

He took his time undressing her, kissing every inch of her body. She felt selfish relishing in his tender touch. Soaking in his attention.

But every time she tried to reciprocate, he patted her hands away, so she gave up, letting him have his way with her.

For the moment.

And boy, did he know how to please her. It was as if he'd been given the user manual to her erogenous zones and how to ignite them so the fire would never go out.

Only, he was an inconvenient flame. One that couldn't last. That was a cold, hard fact she still had to face.

She told herself she wasn't using him because they'd been up front with one another.

As they tangled their arms and legs around each other, getting lost in passion, she pushed all those negative thoughts to the side and focused only on Gael.

Sweet, kind, loving Gael.

He held her in his arms long after their orgasms tore through their bodies like thunder exploding during the worst storm of the season and whispered loving words in her ear.

If she were ever to fall in love.

It would be with a man like Gael.

No.

It would be with Gael.

Only, she couldn't afford to let that happen.

She snuggled in, resting her head on his chest and closing her eyes. She couldn't remember the last time she spent the night with a man.

All night.

"Sleep well," he said softly.

"You too."

"I will with you here."

"Anyone ever tell you that you're corny as hell?"

He chuckled. "No one, actually. This is a new problem that you bring out in me." His lips brushed gently over her temple. "Piper once told me that when you fall for someone, you end up saying the strangest things," he said softly. His chest lifted up slowly and lowered as his breath slowed. If she wasn't mistaken, he'd drifted off to sleep.

Her mind latched on to his words.

Fall for someone...

Another time. Another place.

He'd be it.

10

The old Gael was a selfish prick who only thought about himself. He only did what he wanted and if he did something for someone else, it was because he benefited from it somehow.

He stood over his printer with his hands on his hips and waited for the business plan to finish printing.

Yesterday it had been an idea.

Last night it had been something he might have considered presenting if her deal with Anna fell through.

At three in the morning, he woke in a cold sweat, terrified she'd snuck out and had driven back to New York City.

Thankfully, she'd been blissfully asleep next to him, but that didn't stop him from getting out of bed and running some numbers.

And finishing the plan.

He reached for his coffee mug and took a swig. "Ew." It was cold. He tapped his foot while the last few pages spit out of the machine. He hadn't been this nervous or this excited since he brought in his first client.

That was back when he was green and wasn't chasing the color, but the career. The respect. That was back when he was looking to find exactly what he wanted from a job in finance and he wasn't sure it was being an advisor forever.

He got lost in that rabbit hole.

"Hey, you." Tayla's voice rang out soft and sweet from somewhere in the background. "How long have you been awake?"

He turned, glancing at his watch. "For a while." He pointed to the cup in her hands. "Did you make a fresh pot?"

"I did."

"Thank God." He snagged his mug along with the papers. "We need to talk."

"I don't like the sound of that." She leaned

against the doorjamb wearing only one of his undershirts.

He paused, giving her the once-over. "It's going to be real hard to have any kind of a professional discussion and not rip that shirt off you while taking advantage of you every way I can think of."

"I wouldn't stop you."

He groaned, tucking the paperwork under his arm. "Come on. Let's take this in the kitchen. I've got fresh bagels."

"I say we go back to bed." She climbed up on the stool at the island. "I feel deprived of morning sex."

He chuckled. "We can shower together." He set the papers in front of her, making sure the goal sheets were on top. Then he poured himself a fresh cup of coffee. "After you look at that."

She lifted the stack. "This is at least fifty pages long. How about you give me the abridged version."

"Okay, but you have to promise me that you will hear me out and look at those pages."

"You're being all weird and intense."

The adrenaline racing around his system ran hot and wild. He welcomed it like an old friend. Tentative at first, but then with open arms. The difference this time was it wasn't about hooking the client. Or going in for the kill.

It wasn't about the thrill of it all.

No. This was about finding the thing that could be his future.

About a true partnership.

In more ways than one.

Fear prickled his skin. It was hard to believe he'd fallen this hard. This fast. But that's how most of his life had been. He worried this was a sign his old self was coming to the surface, so he texted Greg, knowing he was working an overnight shift at the hospital.

One of the reasons the boys were at their grandparents.

What Greg had texted back had shocked Gael.

Are you crazy? The old you wouldn't have wanted to help Tayla. He wouldn't have bothered to do a second plan. He certainly wouldn't have considered investing when the risk was that high. You're doing this because you care about her and you believe in her. It's legit. Go for it. But understand she might turn you down.

Gael pressed Greg about his feelings. About the inability to sleep. All of it. Greg told him that normal people felt that way. That normal people got excited about things. That all he was experiencing was the desire and passion to be part of something and someone he wanted to have in his life.

That made sense.

But it frightened Gael.

He could get hurt and that was something he wasn't sure he was prepared for, but as Greg told him, if he didn't take the risk... he'd never get the reward.

"I know. But this has been brewing since I started working on your goal sheets and you've shared with me about your boss and your situation."

"You've got my attention." She set her mug down and leaned back, holding up the first couple of pages. "These are my new goal sheets, which I've only filled in some of the blanks."

"I've taken some liberties with it." He leaned forward, tapping the second sheet. "In that graph I compared the goals that remained the same, and then you can see the things that are different, or left out, and which version they don't show up in."

She turned the page. "Oh. That's interesting." She glanced over the top. "But my end goal, like I've always said, is still the same."

"I know," he said, reaching across the counter and taking one of the sheets and putting it in front of her. "But when you took the job at Anna's, that goal shifted and you know it because you can't have your own line the way you want it with her."

"That's true. But I can make a name for myself so in a couple of years I can leave."

"Except you're trapped." He turned the page. "It's a never-ending cycle. Anna knows it which is why she plays these games." He tapped his finger on the paper. "Do you remember when I said you could use me as the vessel?"

"Yes. But you have yet to explain that."

"The rest of this is a business proposal." Heartburn filled the center of his chest. He scratched at it. "I want to invest in Tayla Johnson Designs. Or whatever you want to call it. And I want to do it by beating Anna at her own game."

"How do you propose we do that?"

He flipped through the pages until he found what he was looking for. "Your contract."

"What about it?"

"The fine print," he said, swaying back and forth. If he wasn't careful, he was going to jump right out of his skin. "You own your designs as long as you can prove they weren't made on company time, by company directive, or created in the office."

"I'm not following." She tucked her hair behind her ears.

"You're on vacation. If you create a line right now, she can't stop you from selling it to anyone."

"But I'm supposed to be sending in a ten-piece collection—"

"Are you telling me you don't have sketches that you could put together that she'd reject?"

"Are you kidding me? She'd ruin my reputation if I did that."

"Not if you had something on the line before she had the chance," Gael said. "And if you had the money to back it." He blew out a puff of air. "That's where I come in."

"My head is spinning and I'm not sure I follow, much less believe we could pull off anything in three days. That's insane."

"Anna would never expect you to do anything like this. She believes you failed the final test. You went on vacation. She wouldn't fathom that you'd use any of that time to put together a collection, pitch it to say Guy Contra, or anyone you want, and beat her at her own game before she had the chance to trash you."

"Would that be legal?"

"As long as you handed in your resignation about the same time Guy signed the contract with me, your business partner." He raised his mug and smiled before taking a sip.

"Doesn't that make me a snake like her?"

Gael let out a long breath. "No. Because from the moment you walk away from Anna Declay Designs, you will be running your business with class. You will respect those who work for you and treat them with kindness."

"And where am I going to have offices? Who am I going to get to work for me?"

"It's all in the business proposal." He made his way around the other side of the counter. He took the papers and set them on the granite. "One of the liberties I took with your goal worksheet was going back to some things you mentioned in the first two."

"And what was that?"

"Owning your own boutique store where you could also buy new up-and-coming designers. Where you could pay it forward. I still own property in New York City. It's been an investment property, but my tenants recently gave me notice and I was going to sell because that was my only tie left to the city."

She palmed his cheek. "No. I can't let you do that. I know how much you need to leave that part of your—"

"I need to help you more." He kissed her lips. They were soft and sweet, and if he never kissed another woman, he'd die a happy man. "I want to do this. And yes, I do have an ulterior motive because I want whatever this is between you and me to be more than two ships passing in the night. I don't know how it will work. If it can work. But I want to try. I'm willing to take a risk. Are you?"

"Wow. That's a lot to take in before the sun rises."

"I know. And I've barely covered the details. One of which you could even eventually live up here."

She lowered her chin and arched both brows. "How could that be possible?"

He leaned over, running his hands over her round ass, across her thighs, and lifting her feet off the ground.

"Whoa." She wrapped her legs around his waist.

"This is where I've completely gone off my rocker. But I'm hoping that we could get the business up and running, and then maybe you can do all your creative work up here. If we're still together."

"Are we a couple now?" she asked.

"I don't let just anyone wash my back."

She laughed. "This is the craziest idea I've ever entertained."

"Are you talking about becoming romantically involved with me? Or being my business partner."

"Both," she said. "But it's the latter one that

makes me the most nervous. What if we can't get Guy, or anyone for that matter to—"

He hushed her with a kiss. "Do you want to be tied to Anna a second longer?"

"No."

"Is she going to screw you regardless?"

"Yes," she said.

"Then you have nothing to lose," he said. "Besides, I want to invest in you regardless. You could walk away from Anna with nothing and a torched reputation and I'd still be there, offering all the same things, because I believe in you. I believe you can be your own brand. Create your line. I know you can do it."

"Gael. Take me to bed or lose me forever."

"Did you just quote, *Top Gun*?"

"Is there a reason we're having the discussion instead of getting naked?"

He hoisted her onto the counter and yanked her panties to her ankles, tossing them over his shoulder. He couldn't care less where they landed. All he cared about was tasting her and making sure he gave her the wickedest orgasm she'd ever experienced.

Nothing else mattered to him at that moment.

He nuzzled himself between her legs.

Her heels dug into his shoulders. His name echoed from her lips.

She hadn't said the words yet, but her excitement came in other ways. They were more than compatible. His fears of being hurt the same way he'd damaged his marriage slowly dissipated into thin air.

It was still a risk.

She could break his heart in two. He knew that and accepted it. However, this was something he needed to do. Not just because he knew he was falling in love with her and it's what his heart wanted, but it's what his soul needed.

This had been the thing he'd been searching for.

His parents would love her.

Piper would adore her and he figured the feeling would be mutual.

"Oh. My God." She threaded her fingers through his hair as she squeezed her thighs together. "Yes. Yes." Her body jerked and twisted. She scooted from the edge of the counter and turned.

Bending her over the island, he slammed into her, gritting his teeth, doing his best to keep some kind of control.

But there was none when it came to Tayla.

He thrust inside her over and over again, his own

climax tearing through his muscles like a boxing match. His lungs burned and he couldn't catch his breath no matter how slowly he inhaled.

Brushing her hair to the side, he kissed her shoulder blade. "Well, now that I've worked up an appetite, we should have some breakfast."

"I'll never look at this counter the same way."

"Me neither."

Ding-dong.

"Shit. Who could that be?" Quickly, he found his shorts and hiked them up over his hips while she pulled her shirt over her head.

"Where are my panties?" she asked.

He glanced around, pretending to fling them over his shoulder again. "They should be over there. But I don't see them. You keep looking. I'll go answer the door." He snagged his coffee and made a beeline for the foyer. At least no one could see back into the kitchen. "Shit. It's your dad."

"Don't answer it," she yelled.

"I can't do that. He can see me," Gael said as he waved and smiled awkwardly at her dad. He leaned forward and opened the door. "Good morning, Tobias."

"Sorry to bother you so early, but I saw the lights on and, well, this is going to be a weird question, but is Tayla here? She's not at home and she's not answering her phone."

Gael swallowed. There was no way for Tayla to sneak upstairs and get her clothes.

Of course, this is what Gael got for his comments last night and being selfish for wanting her to spend the night.

"She's here." Gael could only hope she found her panties. Inwardly, he groaned. What she was wearing wasn't covering much. He lifted his mug and brought it to his lips.

"Thank goodness. We were a little worried, but since her bed wasn't slept in, we figured she crashed here."

Gael coughed, spitting his coffee out on his shirt.

"Are you okay, son?"

"Fine, sir." He pounded his chest. "Let me get Tayla for you." He turned and practically ran toward the kitchen.

Only, Tobias followed him.

"Hi, Daddy," Tayla said, leaning against the counter.

Gael needed an Irish coffee right about now.

"You could have left a note, young lady," Tobias said. "Your mom was worried."

"You knew I was going to come over here early."

She folded her arms. "You didn't need to be the embarrassment committee."

"If you had answered your phone, I wouldn't have come over."

She strolled across the room to where the coffee maker was and lifted her cell. "Not a single missed call, Daddy." She shook her head. "I'm sorry, Gael. I warned you my family could be weird."

"Yes. Yes, you did," Gael said. "Tobias. Would you like a cup of coffee?"

"No. Thanks. But I do have another reason for stopping by," he said. "And I wish it were as fun as watching Gael blush."

"I don't do that, sir," Gael said.

"I've known you for a few months and you've never called me sir. Until now." Tobias shook his head. "Please stop. Just because you and my daughter are having a thing, doesn't mean you and I have to change our friendship. At least I hope we don't."

"Yes, sir. I mean Tobias."

"I'm going to have way too much fun with this," Tobias said. "However, let's get right down to business."

"What's going on, Daddy?" Tayla climbed up on the stool and sipped her coffee.

"I got an email from an old college friend of mine recently who happens to work for a society page in the city." Tobias pulled a piece of paper out of his pocket. He unfolded it and flattened it on the counter. "He's been given an exclusive interview with Anna Declay to discuss a new collection that will be showcased in Guy Contra's Manhattan store. Isn't that going to be your line?"

"Her new collection? Or her new collaboration?" Tayla lifted the paper. Her eyes shifted left and right.

"The only word used was collection," Tobias said.

"So, my gut feeling was right last night. She's going to screw me. And she's going to screw Grace too." Tayla pushed the paper across the counter. "Has this been made public? Why is your friend telling you?"

"Because I told him about you and what's been going on, but that this is all hush-hush. He's not supposed to tell anyone. If it's leaked, he'll lose the exclusivity."

Gael tiptoed around Tobias, making a bold move to wrap his arms around Tayla. He kissed her shoulder. "We knew Anna was up to no good. And we have a plan."

"But based on that, we can't take the designs to

Guy," Tayla said, leaning back into Gael. "And the more I think about it, the more I don't want to."

"Why not?" Gael asked.

She shifted, cupping his face. "Guy's not going to buy me without a big label behind me like Anna. I know that and the thing is I don't want that. What I wanted is the credibility to be able to do it on my own, only that's what I told myself because Matthew was right. I didn't believe I could do it on my own."

"You can, baby girl. I know you can," her father interjected.

"I agree with him."

"Good. Because on Friday morning, I'm going to beat her at her own game," she said. "Daddy. Do you think your friend might be willing to meet with me before he meets with Anna?"

"I can ask," Tobias said.

"Tayla. What are you thinking?" Gael spun the stool so he could get a better look at her facial expressions.

Her eyes lit up like she'd just won her freedom.

"We have a business to plan; that's what I'm thinking."

11

Tayla spent the next twenty-four hours in Gael's house, creating a killer collection.

Or at least she hoped it would be killer.

It was comprised of an everyday line for women. A business casual line for women. Along with a few cocktail dresses.

All designed for the everyday lady.

Nothing too expensive.

That would drive Anna nuts. But it wasn't about Anna. This was about Tayla and her dream. What she'd wanted to do since she'd been in middle school. She glanced over at the goal worksheet. She and Gael had lined up all four of them.

She'd missed the boat when she took the job

with Anna Declay Designs, believing that was the ticket.

Perhaps if she wanted to be a cog in someone else's machine or if she wanted to put her fate in someone else's hands, it would be.

The thing of it was she never set out to be the top one percent. Success was measured in so many different ways and she'd forgotten that.

But this new collection was a year away from being in stores. In her store.

That thought gave her goosebumps. Granted, it was going to be a very small boutique. And she was going to have to fill it with other designers. But she'd be able to pick and choose.

And she'd listen to her clients. Who they wanted.

She'd finally be in control.

Meanwhile, she was prepared to turn in her final ten pieces, under her current contract with Anna Declay Designs. She had an old lawyer friend of Gael's going over the contract one last time to make sure they weren't missing anything, but what she was about to do would sting Anna.

More importantly, it would make it so Anna couldn't sting her back.

"How's it going?" Gael placed a glass of wine on the desk.

"I think I'm done. Do you want to see?" She turned the computer screen and leaned back.

"Wow. I don't know anything about women's fashion. But those are beautiful," he said. "It's a shame you have to give them to Anna."

"It's the only way."

"I get it, but still." He nodded. "These are amazing, and I hate that she'll own them."

"I have more of these in me."

"I'm so glad to hear you talk this way."

"You know, you don't have to come with me tomorrow. I know going into the city is the last thing you want to do."

"I want to be there for you. For us."

"Speaking of us. We still need a name for this business," she said.

"What about your name? I thought that's what most designers did." He took a step back and leaned against the wall, sipping his wine. "And we have time. Our business technically has nothing to do with sticking it to Anna. She doesn't need to know anything about it. At least not from our mouths. We'll leave that up to your dad's buddy."

She'd given this a lot of thought over the last day while she'd been working, staring at his sister's paintings, which had been the inspiration for the new collection. Piper was everywhere in this house.

Tayla felt her in her heart. Her soul. It was as if she'd guided her designs.

"I want to show you something." She tapped on the keyboard and pulled up the preliminary drawings. They needed work, but a couple pieces were close to being completed.

"Those are cool." He leaned closer. "My God. They remind me of my sister."

"I feel like she's in my head. I know that's weird. I never met her, but she's the inspiration for all of these."

He blew out a puff of air as he ran a hand over his eyes. "I don't know what to say."

"How would you feel if I called the very first collection, *The Piper Collection*."

His hand came down on the desk. "Are you serious?"

"I don't have to if you don't want me to. And I understand you might need to run this by Greg."

"I will need to ask him, but personally, I think it's incredible."

"That brings me to the company name."

"I'm afraid to ask." He pulled up a chair.

"Tayla & Piper Creations." She climbed up on his

lap. "Whatever store space we have, I'd like her paintings everywhere." Tears filled her eyes.

And Gael's.

She pressed her hand on Gael's chest. "I know you probably think I'm nuts. And I understand if you and Greg—"

Gael pressed his finger over her mouth. "I love it. We'll take it to Greg. If he's on board, that's the name."

"We're doing this business, aren't we?"

He nodded. "We're also falling in love."

12

Gael set his overnight bag on the dresser in Tayla's bedroom. He meandered to the window and stared out at the city below.

He couldn't believe he was back.

Even if for only one night.

He leaned against the glass and watched the cars whiz by eight stories below in the city that never slept. He had experienced that firsthand. His heart pounded against his rib cage. It was painful, making it challenging to take a full breath.

"Sorry, this place is such a mess," Tayla said as she stepped from the bathroom, tugging at her robe. "I find it ironic that my lease renewal was in my mailbox."

"If all goes as planned tomorrow, you will have thirty days to vacate the premises." He turned. "How do you feel about that?"

"I spend so little time here that I can't say I will miss it. But honestly, the idea that I will be moving back home with Mommy and Daddy isn't sitting well with me." She fell back on the mattress, spreading her arms wide.

His emotions ran hot when it came to Tayla. At his core, they were a fireball that filled his gut and spread out through his system, taking over his every waking thought. Not to mention she crept into his dreams.

During the last hour in the car, all he could think about while she took a catnap was how much he cared for her and wanted to build a future. He could see what it looked like. Taste the sweetness of it. Feel the love it created.

It was exactly what his sister had described.

"That's temporary." He sat on the edge of the bed, running his fingers through her long hair. "Besides, something tells me you'll be spending most of your time with me."

She lifted her head. "That is a nice perk." She rolled to her side. "Not that I need to define this, but I literally turned my life upside down. I have no idea what I'm doing or if it will be successful. Also, Anna could still find a way to screw me over. This thing between us is happening so fast and furious I can't think straight."

"I know the feeling." When he called Greg to discuss his future plans, Greg had some concerns about how tightly woven Gael's life had become with Tayla's so quickly. Greg wasn't suggesting that he stop, or even pump the brakes. But he wanted Gael to remember all the things that he'd been worried about and to make sure he had his mind in the right place when dealing with business.

And romance.

"Are we crazy?" she asked.

"We might be a little bit."

"Are you okay?" She scooted closer, resting her head on his lap. "The closer we got to the city, the quieter you became."

"This is the first time I've been back since I moved and I'll be honest. Outside of being there for you tomorrow, I don't want to be here. I'm struggling with being back in this city in more ways than one."

She reached out and rubbed her soft hand across his cheek. "Are you worried I'm going to get bored and want to come back to this life?"

"That thought has crossed my mind."

"You've shown me how I can have it all. You've helped me see what my family has been trying to remind me of for the last year, and I'm bristling with excitement." She shifted, straddling his lap. "I can't wait to start calling people I know in the business. Smaller designers. People who are looking for a shot. We're going to fill our boutique store with artists. People who need that break. The ones who didn't get it because they had to work under bitches like Anna. Or who are struggling to maintain more than one dream."

His heart swelled. "Piper would have loved you."

"I wish I could have known her," Tayla whispered as her lips gently swept over his mouth.

She tasted like sweetness on a roll. This tightness he felt in the center of his chest came from the mixture of his deep feelings for her and his fear of being back in the city.

He smelled the money the moment they got off the highway. He immediately started salivating. His pulse soared to new heights.

But none of it was positive and it didn't give him a good feeling.

He knew he still had to be careful. Greed still flowed in his veins.

At least now he knew what that emotion felt like

and he could hopefully control it. He suspected that this business partnership would bring him into the city a few more times.

He needed to be stronger.

For himself.

And for Tayla.

As long as he could get through tomorrow, he could get through anything. That would be his test. All he had to do was go in and be there for Tayla. Support her and open his mouth only when it was called for.

The kiss quickly deepened. He needed Tayla as much as she needed him and that was a reality that eased his soul.

Piper told him on her wedding day that love required a lot of things and that she knew she and Greg would make the long haul because they weren't ashamed to admit they needed one another.

Back then, he thought that was bullshit.

But right now?

This moment?

It made perfect sense.

As they tumbled back on the bed, stripping each other of their clothing, desperate to please one another, all his fear dissipated like the night sky gave way to the morning sun, and he accepted that he'd fallen in love in the Adirondacks in a weekend.

He didn't need to share that piece of information with the object of his affection.

Yet.

No reason to scare her off.

After they were spent from their lovemaking, he held her in his arms and stared at the ceiling.

With Tayla in his life, he believed he could find that balance in life that he wished he'd had before his family had died. But what he also understood was that no matter what, even if he could go back in time and make different choices, they might still be gone.

Life was full of risks, heartbreak, and happiness.

He'd experienced it all and Piper and his parents were looking down on him now, smiling, knowing that he'd finally listened.

13

Friday morning came too fast and Tayla found herself wanting to crawl right out of her skin.

She was in over her head and she knew it.

"Relax." Gael took her hand. "This is going to be the easy part."

"I wish I believed that." She pointed to Matthew as he made his way across the lobby of Anna Declay Designs. "I hate springing this on him."

"We couldn't risk anyone finding out what you were planning on doing."

"I thought this was a *we* program," she said.

He leaned in and kissed her cheek. "It is. But I don't work here and our business needs to be protected. I know you want to bring him over and

I'm on board with that. But not until after all your exit papers are signed."

She glanced at her watch. "That won't happen for at least a half hour."

"Can you keep a poker face that long?"

"Not with you sticking your tongue in my ear." She squared her shoulders and prepared to face Matthew and all his questions.

"My goodness, girl. Who is this man and why have you been keeping him a secret? Is it because you think I'll try to steal him from you?"

"Matthew. Meet Gael, and yes. That's exactly it," she said.

"It's nice to finally meet you." Gael stretched out his arm. "I've heard so much about you."

"I wish I could say the same." Matthew glared.

"Sometimes I want to keep things to myself. Like my private life." She'd never in a million years lie to Matthew.

Yet she just did.

She had to. She'd beg him for forgiveness in about an hour or so when she was able to offer him a job in her new business.

Tayla and Piper Creations.

God. She loved how that rolled off her tongue, even if she was only thinking the words.

Even more so that Greg had approved of the entire concept. The fact that he was on board and that he even agreed to a children's line someday made her heart sing. It was all she could hope for.

Now all she had to do was make both Greg and Gael proud.

But first she had to get through this meeting with Anna.

"As much as I'd love to stand here and shoot the shit with this hunk of man, Anna is waiting for you in the main room," Matthew said. "Gael can wait here."

"Gael will be coming with us," Tayla said.

Matthew jerked his head back. "Girl. Have you lost your ever-loving mind? Are you looking to get fired? Have we not been talking strategy over getting your own line?"

"I need you to trust me," Tayla said. "Can you do that?"

"No offense. It's not you I don't trust," Matthew said.

"I'm not offended by that." Gael laced his fingers through Tayla's. "I would be concerned about me if I were you as well. But I want you to know I have only Tayla's best interests at heart."

"Doesn't matter what I think. I'm here to support

my girl. If she wants you in this meeting, who am I to argue? But before we go in, you need to know it all went down with Grace. It wasn't pretty. As a matter of fact, it was damn freaking ugly and Grace is cleaning out her desk right now."

"What happened?" Tayla asked. "Did she get fired? Quit?"

"She was fired. For cause," Matthew said. "Anna had been keeping track of all the things she'd broken in her design contract. Everything that Grace did—even if it was a directive given by Anna through someone else—had been documented and kept in a file. But Anna acted as though she had no idea that Grace was going to come at her with her designs for Guy Contra today."

"But didn't you say there were two meetings in Anna's calendar?" Tayla asked. "And what about all the meetings Anna and Grace were having?"

"It wasn't about Guy Contra. That's for sure," Matthew said. "When Anna called all the designers onto the main floor, she started off all smiles and was bubbling with excitement. She started off talking about how Guy Contra had been talking to her about a collection for his Manhattan store. Grace was out of her seat and hooking up her computer to the projection screen. She honestly believed, and with good reason, that she was going to be showing off her collection."

Tayla looped her hand into the crook of Matthew's arm as they strolled toward the elevator. "Did Anna let her start her presentation?"

"Anna acted stunned and speechless, and then she laid into her like no tomorrow. I couldn't help but feel horrible for Grace. No one deserves to be set up and treated that way. Anna actually pulled out a piece of paper and read at least ten items where Grace broke her employee contract, and then she fired her, but only after she reminded her that those designs were the property of Anna Declay Designs," Matthew said.

"I can't believe what a fool I've been," Tayla mumbled.

"Don't go there." Gael squeezed her shoulder. "Focus on our plan."

"What plan?" Matthew asked. "What is this tall drink of something talking about?"

"First, thank you for the compliment," Gael said. "But it's best if you just follow along and let Tayla do what she set out to."

"It's not in my nature to be silent, but I can follow a lead." Matthew hit the button to the fifth floor. "If I don't speak, Anna might think something is up.

She's already going to be wondering who the hell the eye candy is."

"I'm exactly that. Eye candy. Here to make sure my girlfriend continues to get her vacation."

"Why do I think there's more to this story than that?" Matthew said as they climbed into the elevator. "I can't believe you're really not going to fill me in."

She opened her mouth, but Gael covered it with his hand. "Please, follow our lead."

Matthew raised his hand. "Whatever my girl needs, I've got her back."

The elevator doors closed.

Tayla squared her shoulders. This was it. Their entire plan was riding on the next few minutes.

"It's going to be fine," Gael whispered. "Me throwing her off her game is going to be the icing on the cake."

Tayla still wasn't sold on that little piece of the puzzle, but she wasn't about to ask Gael to leave. She needed his support. His fingers intertwined with hers like a tightly woven sweater. The idea that they could be partners—in everything—for the rest of their lives made her soul sing.

She remembered writing her second goal worksheet with her grandfather and making room in her life for a husband.

Children.

A family.

She'd pushed those thoughts out of her mind around the time she'd started pursuing working for a major designer and getting her own line that way. Somehow, all her hopes and dreams had twisted and morphed into a singular thought.

That had all changed the moment she met Gael.

When he'd mentioned falling in love, she thought her heart had stopped beating. She knew she'd been *falling* for him. But she hadn't thought that meant love.

But that's exactly what that meant.

And now she lived for the idea.

Nothing was set in stone. Everything was up in the air. It was scary. She honestly didn't know what her future looked like, but she knew without a doubt, Gael would be in it.

Tayla cleared her mind of all the white noise and focused on the plan. What she and Gael rehearsed on the drive to her apartment last night and over coffee on the subway to the office.

The elevator jerked to a stop and the doors opened.

Grace stood on the other side, tears streaming down her cheeks. She looked up and gasped.

Tayla shouldn't care that Anna destroyed Grace's self-esteem and career with only a few words, but she did.

"Anna is waiting for you," Grace managed through a few broken sobs.

"I'm so sorry about what happened. Are you okay?" Tayla asked.

Grace glared.

"Damn, girl. I'm sorry," Matthew said. "*But seriously, that's classic I'm going to fuck with you*, Anna."

"Thanks for the reminder that I just got played." Grace blew out a puff of air. "And that you don't like me."

"That's not true," Tayla said. "Anna pit us against one another." She waved her hand toward the main floor. "She's made this entire company an adversarial place to work. She thrives on conflict."

"That's very true. And we've all been waiting to see which one of us was going to be humiliated. Looks like it was me. I don't think she'll do it twice in one day."

"Why don't you stick around and find out," Tayla said, squeezing Gael's hand, wishing her thoughts could be transported through her skin.

Grace's talent couldn't be denied. Nor could a few other designers who had been humiliated, fired, or simply quit because of the way Anna treated people. They all deserved a chance. The one that Anna had stolen from them because of her own inadequate feelings.

"It was bad enough to have to walk out of the room after she shamed me in front of everyone. But to watch her praise you…" Grace shook her head. "…I'm sorry. No offense. You deserve this break. I know that. I can't sit here and watch it."

"Trust me. You're going to want to," Gael said. "It's not what you think."

"Who are you?" Grace narrowed her stare.

"The boyfriend." He smiled proudly. "Come on. This is going to be fun."

"Your boyfriend is oddly adorable," Grace whispered. "And I don't know why I'm staying. All it's going to do is give people something more to whisper about tomorrow."

"Um, Gael," Matthew started. "You don't know how things work around here and not to be a mean girl, but Grace is a mean girl and shouldn't have a seat at our table."

"He's right," Grace said. "I have been a total bitch."

"I believe you're a victim in all this." Gael pressed his hand on Tayla's back and nudged her forward, toward the design floor, where everyone had gathered. The entire team was there, sitting in folding chairs in front of a screen.

Anna stood off to the side near a podium. She glanced up just as Tayla approached. Anna glanced at her wrist. "You're a few minutes early," she said. "And you brought... Who is that handsome gentleman?"

"This is Gael," Tayla said. "He's my boyfriend and he's here to observe and for moral support."

Anna tilted her head and pursed her lips.

She was not amused.

"He can't stay," Anna said, planting her hands on his hips. "We have copyrighted designs. We don't need our competitors—"

"He signed all the necessary paperwork at the front desk," Tayla started.

"I don't care." Anna slowly stepped to the other side of the podium. Her movement was methodical. She didn't show concern. Or any emotion. "Your collection is due today and I wanted to examine it with the team." So, she had planned a public shaming. Even though Tayla's designs were top notch, Anna was going to find something wrong with them.

Knowing her, she had a directive sheet from Guy for the collection and it wasn't anything like what she expressed to Tayla. That would make it easy for her to tear the designs apart because they wouldn't meet customer expectation. It didn't matter that Tayla didn't know what those were. "I don't want him here and I want to see your designs right now." Anna pointed to the projector. "I was supposed to have them in my inbox by ten. You'll be breaking a clause in your employee contract if you don't turn those in."

Tayla patted her briefcase. "I actually sent them five minutes ago." Tayla sucked in a deep breath. She needed all the strength she could muster. "But I see no point in a showing unless it's to the client that it was designed for."

"I'm not sure what you're talking about." Anna folded her arms.

"We discussed how Guy Contra was looking for—"

Anna shook her head, holding up her hand. "I don't know how we could have discussed that since he literally just sent over his specifications to me this week and part of this meeting today was to go over with the design team what he's looking for. This collection will be a group project. I'm expecting everyone to contribute." She jerked her hip out and waved a hand in front of her face. "I was hoping your sketches might start us off. But this little temper tantrum isn't a good look on you."

"Maybe this would be a good time for us to discuss my future in private. Not in front of the entire team." Tayla's toes and fingertips went numb. Even though she knew she'd be able to walk out of this building and start her own boutique along with her own clothing line, that didn't help her nerves.

"Your future? You just shot yourself in the foot." Anna strolled across the room with her head held high, a slight smile on her face. More like a cocky smirk.

All the designers either shifted their stare between Anna and Tayla or they kept their head down, eyes focused on the floor, waiting for the bomb to drop. They knew better than to leave. Anyone who did would get penalized.

"I don't believe I did." This wasn't going exactly as planned, but it would work. She glanced toward Gael, who nodded. She filled her lungs with oxygen. Holding her breath for a few moments, she collected her thoughts. She exhaled as she dug into her purse. "And I don't think we want to do this here. In front of everyone."

"Oh, Tayla. Don't threaten me," Anna said.

"This isn't a threat." Tayla pulled out a manila envelope from her briefcase. "This is my letter of resignation, ending my employment today. Or you can try to fire me. Up to you."

"You can't just quit," Anna said. "There are procedures. Legalities that need to be followed."

"She's already taken care of them," Gael said.

Anna looked him up and down. "Unless there is a noncompete agreement and a nondisclosure agreement in there, you can't walk out of here today."

"Oh. But she can." Gael took the papers from Tayla's trembling hands. "These were drawn up by a lawyer. They are standard. You can keep the designs she'd worked on this past week. She won't discuss the terms of her leaving Anna Declay Designs. And neither will you."

Anna snatched the papers from Gael's hands.

He smiled.

"She's already signed that one. All you have to do is sign it. The noncompete states she won't work for a designer who has an office in New York City for the term of two years."

"No one is going to hire her anyway after they hear what a backstabbing diva she is," Anna muttered.

"But you can't discuss my leaving." Tayla found her voice, and it was strong. Powerful. "Or the reasons around it. We've come up with a couple different announcements you can make about why I left that are acceptable. But outside of that, neither one of us can trash the other. Ever. And—" Tayla held up her finger. "Because you chose to do this in front of everyone, I get to inform them that they too can protect themselves from your bad business practices."

"How dare you," Anna exclaimed. "I will not stand here and be spoken to like this by you."

Gael handed Anna a pen. "Sign on the dotted line and we'll be glad to leave."

"I need to have my legal team look at these."

"We emailed them to Human Resources and the legal department. We'll wait," Gael said as he leaned against one of the desks and folded his arms. "But if we walk out that door without you signing, Tayla will email her designs to Guy, which she can do based on your employee—"

"That would be breaking her contract. I could fire her and sue her if she did that." Anna made a *tsk* noise. "You really should do your homework."

Gael laughed. "I have. And I had a friend of mine get in touch with a fashion lawyer who examined your contract with Tayla. Went over every single word. Every single clause. And the second you acknowledged that you had an appointment lined up with the customer to look at a line designed by Tayla was the moment you—"

"I did no such thing." Anna slammed her hand on the table next to her.

"I have the messages to prove it." Tayla held up her phone. "Granted, I'm the one who used his name, but you confirmed the meeting. Now, I'm happy to walk away. Today. I just need you to sign and you never have to lay eyes on me again." Tayla dared to smile.

"In my office. Now." Anna turned on her heel and stormed off.

"Damn, girl," Matthew said, fanning himself. "That was ridiculously awesome."

"There's a lot I can't tell you standing right here, but I have a plan and I want you to be part of it." For the first time in two years, Tayla felt like she was actually in charge of her own career. Her own destiny.

And damn, that felt fantastic.

She turned to Grace. "You too."

"You're my flipping hero," Grace said. "I can't

believe we all take the kind of abuse we have from her."

"Because we love our jobs and we want to see our creations in stores and ultimately in people's closets. Anna feeds on our dreams," Tayla said. "But I'm not giving her mine anymore." She slipped her arm around Gael's waist. "We better go make sure she signs those."

"Lead the way."

This was it. This was the beginning of her future.

∽

Tayla held her breath while Anna sat behind her desk and tapped her pen on the tabletop. Someone from the legal department held a copy of the papers as he leaned on the corner of the desk while he rubbed his temple.

Gael sipped water by the door while she did her best not to freak out.

"I want five years not working for a designer in New York City, and that means anyone with an office here."

"That's unreasonable," Gael said. "Three years."

"All right." Anna sighed. "I'm so disappointed in you, Tayla. I thought we were a team."

"We were never that," Tayla said. "And you never had any intention of breaking me out and giving me my own line. So let's stop pretending."

Anna licked the tip of the pen and signed both sets of documents as the lawyer initialed them. "I will honor this, but if you even breathe a bad word about me in this town or with anyone I work with, I will crush you."

"I'm well aware of how you work." Tayla stood and stretched out her hand. "I'll take my copy and will vacate the premises now."

"You're making a huge mistake." Anna leaned forward and clasped her hands together. "You will never make it in this town now."

"We'll see about that." She tucked the papers into her briefcase and took Gael by the hand. "Are you ready?"

"I sure am."

They made their way down the long corridor in silence. The only thing she could hear was her heart beating between her ears.

"Are you okay?" Gael asked once they were in the elevator, heading down to the main floor.

"I'll be honest. I'm scared."

"I'd be worried about you if you weren't."

"I can't believe I just did that." She wrapped her

arms around Gael and rested her head on his shoulder. "I'm unemployed, and I'm going to be moving home with my parents."

Gael tilted her chin. "First. You're not unemployed. You're starting your own business. Second, isn't it going to be nice that you will be living next door to your boyfriend?"

She smiled. "That is a bonus. And we'll be working together."

"The first thing we should do is make sure you actually take a little time off and enjoy the time you promised your family." He batted her nose. "And now me."

"Look at you bossing me around already."

"I'm going to make one more request," he said.

"Yeah. What's that?"

"Can we please get the hell out of this city? It's making me twitch."

She rose up on tiptoe. "Only if you promise to take me sailing when we get home."

"You are so demanding."

"You have no idea." What started out as an inconvenient flame turned into a possible lifetime of fire.

14

ONE MONTH LATER...

Gael leaned against the doorjamb of the potential storefront. So much had happened. He'd been lucky to have found a buyer for his property in the city, making all of this that much easier. He was ready to buy the entire building, but he'd leave that decision up to his business partner. "Well?" However, he was a bit impatient at the moment.

Not because they had to sign on the dotted line right this second. They didn't. But because her family, his nephews, and Greg were all waiting for them in the parking lot. Of course, it would all suck if she said no.

They had not discussed much this side of their future, other than they loved each other and she was moving in with him this weekend. That made the most sense since she spent most nights at his house with the exception of her *sleepovers* with her sisters.

Something that he'd never take away from her and he would continue to encourage her to have those special moments with her sisters.

"I like it," she said, nodding her head as she spun in a circle in the center with her arms out wide. "I think it's perfect."

"Good. Why don't we go out to dinner, discuss the logistics, and sign the paperwork."

She ran toward him, crashing into his body.

"Umph." He gripped her hips.

"This is really happening, isn't it?"

"It sure is." He wrapped his arms around her waist. "I'm so proud of everything you've managed to accomplish in the last few weeks."

"It's all because I have you and my family in my corner."

"Perhaps that helps, but this is all you. Your talent. You're amazing, and I love you."

She tilted her head. "I love you right back."

"Yeah." He kissed her nose, taking a step back, stuffing his hand in his pocket. "Do you love me enough to marry me?" He pulled out the diamond ring he'd purchased yesterday. He'd gotten the stamp of approval from Greg and her two sisters. Not just on him popping the question, but on the ring itself. "Because I love you more than words could ever express."

"Oh, my God." She blinked. "Are you serious?"

"No. I thought I'd fake propose for shits and giggles." He took her hand and pushed the ring on her finger. "It fits, so I'm hoping I don't have to stand here like an idiot much longer because our families are waiting for us so they can either celebrate or talk me from jumping in the lake."

"Well, the latter won't be necessary," she said with a beaming smile and tears rolling down her cheeks. "Of course, I'll marry you."

He took her chin with his thumb and forefinger. "Do you think your sister will give us the wedding planner discount?"

"Oh, she better. And she better find a way to have Foster get us a deal on that wedding boat ride because that shit is expensive, and we're on a budget."

There was nothing better than being in love in the Adirondacks.

Thank you for taking the time to read AN INCONVENIENT FLAME. I would so appreciate it if you could leave an honest review and tell your friends about the series. That is the best gift any reader can give to an author. If you haven't picked up the next two books in the series, please do! SHATTERED DREAMS is Tiki's story and THE WEDDING DRIVER is Tonya's. Thank you so much. Readers rule!

GRAB A GLASS OF VINO, kick back, relax, and let the romance roll in...

SIGN up for my Newsletter (https://dl.bookfunnel.com/82gm8b9k4y) where I often give away free books before publication.

JOIN my private Facebook group (https://www.facebook.com/groups/191706547909047/) where I post exclusive excerpts and discuss all things murder and love!

ABOUT THE AUTHOR

Jen Talty is the *USA Today* Bestselling Author of Contemporary Romance, Romantic Suspense, and Paranormal Romance. In the fall of 2020, her short story was selected and featured in a 1001 Dark Nights Anthology.

Regardless of the genre, her goal is to take you on a ride that will leave you floating under the sun with warmth in your heart. She writes stories about broken heroes and heroines who aren't necessarily looking for romance, but in the end, they find the kind of love books are written about :).

She first started writing while carting her kids to one hockey rink after the other, averaging 170 games per year between 3 kids in 2 countries and 5 states. Her first book, IN TWO WEEKS was originally published in 2007. In 2010 she helped form a publishing company (Cool Gus Publishing) with *NY*

Times Bestselling Author Bob Mayer where she ran the technical side of the business through 2016.

Jen is currently enjoying the next phase of her life... the empty nester! She and her husband reside in Jupiter, Florida.

Grab a glass of vino, kick back, relax, and let the romance roll in...

Sign up for my Newsletter (https://dl.bookfunnel.com/82gm8b9k4y) where I often give away free books before publication.

Join my private Facebook group (https://www.facebook.com/groups/191706547909047/) where I post exclusive excerpts and discuss all things murder and love!

Never miss a new release. Follow me on Amazon:amazon.com/author/jentalty

And on Bookbub: bookbub.com/authors/jentalty

ALSO BY JEN TALTY

Check out LOVE IN THE ADIRONDACKS!

AN INCONVENIENT FLAME

SHATTERED DREAMS

THE WEDDING DRIVER

Brand new series: SAFE HARBOR!

MINE TO KEEP

MINE TO SAVE

MINE TO PROTECT

Colorado Brotherhood Protectors

Defending Raven

Fay's Six

Yellowstone Brotherhood Protectors

Defending Payton

Legacy Series

Dark Legacy

Legacy of Lies

Secret Legacy

Candlewood Falls

RIVERS EDGE

THE BURIED SECRET

ITS IN HIS KISS

LIPS OF AN ANGEL

With Me In Seattle

INVESTIGATE WITH ME

SAIL WITH ME

FLY WITH ME

The Monroes

COLOR ME YOURS

COLOR ME SMART

COLOR ME FREE

COLOR ME LUCKY

COLOR ME ICE

It's all in the Whiskey

JOHNNIE WALKER

GEORGIA MOON

JACK DANIELS

JIM BEAM

WHISKEY SOUR

WHISKEY COBBLER

WHISKEY SMASH

Search and Rescue

PROTECTING AINSLEY

PROTECTING CLOVER

PROTECTING OLYMPIA

PROTECTING FREEDOM

PROTECTING PRINCESS

NY STATE TROOPER SERIES

In Two Weeks

Dark Water

Deadly Secrets

Murder in Paradise Bay

To Protect His own

Deadly Seduction

When A Stranger Calls

His Deadly Past

The Corkscrew Killer

Brand New Novella for the First Responders series

A spin off from the NY State Troopers series

PLAYING WITH FIRE

PRIVATE CONVERSATION

THE RIGHT GROOM

AFTER THE FIRE

CAUGHT IN THE FLAMES

DELTA FORCE-NEXT GENERATION

SHIELDING JOLENE

SHIELDING AALYIAH

SHIELDING LAINE

The Men of Thief Lake

REKINDLED

DESTINY'S DREAM

Federal Investigators

JANE DOE'S RETURN

THE BUTTERFLY MURDERS

The Aegis Network

THE LIGHTHOUSE

HER LAST HOPE

THE LAST FLIGHT

THE RETURN HOME

THE MATRIARCH

Special Forces Operation Alpha

BURNING DESIRE

BURNING KISS

BURNING SKIES

BURNING LIES

BURNING HEART

BURNING BED

REMEMBER ME ALWAYS

The Brotherhood Protectors

Out of the Wild

ROUGH JUSTICE

ROUGH AROUND THE EDGES

ROUGH RIDE

ROUGH EDGE

ROUGH BEAUTY

The Brotherhood Protectors

The Saving Series

SAVING LOVE

SAVING MAGNOLIA

SAVING LEATHER

Hot Hunks

Cove's Blind Date Blows Up

My Everyday Hero – Ledger

Tempting Tavor

Malachi's Mystic Assignment

Needing Neor

Holiday Romances

A CHRISTMAS GETAWAY

<u>ALASKAN CHRISTMAS</u>

WHISPERS

CHRISTMAS IN THE SAND

CHRISTMAS IN JULY

Heroes & Heroines on the Field

TAKING A RISK

TEE TIME

A New Dawn

THE BLIND DATE

SPRING FLING

SUMMERS GONE

WINTER WEDDING

The Collective Order

THE LOST SISTER

THE LOST SOLDIER

THE LOST SOUL

THE LOST CONNECTION

A Spin-Off Series: Witches Academy Series

THE NEW ORDER